Metropolitan Political Analysis

A
SOCIAL
ACCESS
APPROACH

Oliver P. Williams

AN ARKVILLE PRESS BOOK

THE FREE PRESS, NEW YORK
COLLIER-MACMILLAN LIMITED, LONDON

The Free Press
A DIVISION OF THE MACMILLAN COMPANY
866 Third Avenue, New York, New York 10022
Collier-Macmillan Canada Ltd., Toronto, Ontario
Library of Congress Catalog Card Number: 70–136275
       Printing Number
1 2 3 4 5 6 7 8 9 10

4.95/EEE/1

METROPOLITAN
POLITICAL
ANALYSIS

FOREWORD

The annual Clarke A. Sanford Lectures on Local Government and Community Life were established at the State University Agricultural and Technical College at Delhi, New York, by his son and colleague, Roswell Sanford, and long-time friend, Armand G. Erpf, a senior partner of Loeb, Rhoades and Company, New York, to perpetuate the memory of Clarke A. Sanford. For sixty years Sanford was editor and publisher of the "Catskill Mountain News," a rural upstate New York newspaper. Designed to stimulate research and scholarship, each lecture was, and is, expanded into a book for the purpose of enriching the literature of the social sciences.

In the 1968 Sanford Lecture, Dr. Oliver Williams, Professor and Chairman of the Department of Political Science at the University of Pennsylvania, made his audience keenly aware of the multiplicity of approaches being employed by social scientists studying and exploring urban problems. He offered substantial evidence to support the view that neither a coherent theoretical framework for urban study nor adequate data for policy formulation could emerge unless social scientists began to treat "urbanism" as a conceptually distinct social and political process. In this volume he elaborated this view, mounted additional evidence, and proposed guidelines which social scientists should find of real value in constructing a conceptual framework. Decision-makers and laymen will also find this book a penetrating and

FOREWORD (cont.)

comprehensible exposition of the multi-dimensional nature of the problems and needs of an urban society.

Recently, a collection of Clarke Sanford's newspaper columns written during the nineteen-forties and fifties and edited by his grandson, Lawrence Anderson of Binghamton, New York, came to my attention. This collection reveals the deep perception of this rural man. Clarke Sanford never lost sight of the fact that his own community of Margaretville and hundreds like it stretching across the U. S. were getting closer and closer to the hearts of rapidly expanding population centers. He knew that the technological revolution would no longer allow rural areas to exist in the splendid isolation of years gone by, and that problems of the urban American would affect and alter the character of rural America.

Clarke Sanford would not have been intimidated by the idea of "metropolitan government," understanding as he did that places, like people, could not be isolated islands in troubled seas. The idea of both "new wine" and "new bottles" was to be encouraged and nourished if it were to solve problems, enrich the quality of living, and protect individual liberty.

Seldon M. Kruger
Professor and Chairman
Division of Arts and Sciences
State University of New York
Agricultural and Technical College
Delhi, New York

CONTENTS

PREFACE

Book previewers may be divided into two classes, those who try to find what a book is about by reading the jacket, table of contents, and introduction, and those who start in the middle and leaf both ways. The first group assumes that authors are systematic and orderly in their mode of presentation; the latter are skeptics. I personally fall into the latter class, but I happen to admire the assumptions of the former. Therefore, I will try to characterize accurately this book here at the outset.

The intended audiences are, first, political scientists who engage in urban studies, second, urban scholars generally, and third, those with a general interest in urban affairs. The last group may find a few chapters that drag, but I encourage them to persevere to the latter portion of the book. Those urbanists who identify themselves with geography and ecology will find much that is familiar and some that is less so. I hope it will be helpful to all who are interested in urban politics.

The volume is conceptual and normative. It contains little new data. It talks of models, but falls short of theory building. This admission is made somewhat apologetically, because we have many conceptual statements in print, the value of which is rarely subjected to empirical tests. This author's only defense is that most of his previous work has involved analysis of data, at times with an inadequate framework, and perhaps the right has been earned to engage in this more speculative venture. The book is normative in that the conceptual model, if valid, has very obvious policy implications. The plausibility of the model is argued, and its policy relevance is spelled out.

My immediate reason for this project stems from my dismay in trying to relate to other political scientists who are presumably working on urban politics. The heterogeneity of their interests and the disparate nature of urban studies adds up to an eclectically assembled heap of disorganized observations. This result is not a function of the complexity of the subject matter, but of our own confusion. My intention is to start a discussion which will focus on treating urbanism as a conceptually distinct social and political process. I hope we will be able to identify a set of questions worth asking.

This volume was made possible largely through the support of the Clarke A. Sanford Lecture Fund of the College Association at Delhi, Inc., and the Social Science Research Council. I wish to thank those associated with both of these undertakings for their support. I want to commend Seldon Kruger of the State University of New York at Delhi for his patience and understanding toward broken promises on my part regarding deadlines for delivering this manuscript.

Of the many people who contributed to my ideas in writing this volume, Thomas Anton certainly ranks foremost. His comments led me to revise the original manuscript extensively, and I believe it is a much clearer statement as a result of his suggestions. James Q. Wilson also read the original manuscript, and his helpful comments are most appreciated. I have benefited from discussions with countless graduate students in various classes and seminars over the past several years. Many of my ideas come from written sources, and while I have tried to follow footnoting credit conventions, I fear that memory's pranks may have led me to take credit for many ideas which properly should be given to others.

Finally, I would like to express my thanks and appreciation to my wife, Marion, not simply for her help in unsnarling my involuted grammatical style, but for just being herself.

O. P. W.

Philadelphia, 1970

Chapter 1

POLITICS
AND
URBANISM

The search for the "essence" of urbanism is an old one, and one which has been more commonly engaged in by sociologists, geographers, and historians than by political scientists. This conceptual omission by political scientists has led them to overlook the most fundamental urban political acts and to be superficial in the portrayal of the urban political process. This problem is particularly acute with reference to the American experience, where particularism and decentralization obfuscates politics from the purview of laymen as well as political scientists. While the former may be excused, the latter may not, for it is their vocation to strip away the mysteries imbedded in complex political arrangements. This volume endeavors to fashion a concept which will enable us to see that which is often omitted in urban politics.

Two general approaches have been employed in conceptualizing urbanism: one identifies it as a way of life, and the other employs spatial language. Political scientists have generally looked to the former tradition, while the latter actually provides a better starting point. However, when political scientists have used spatial notions, they have done so in a fashion which limits rather than furthers inquiry.

The principal difficulties with the way-of-life approach is that its ideas are heavily influenced by the historical conditions surrounding their development. Sociologists whose observations coincided with the huge urbanization push brought about by nineteenth-century technology tended to identify urbanization

1

2

Metropolitan Political Analysis

with the behavior manifest when a rural population was shifted
to a radically different social milieu. The heterogeneity and complexity of city, as opposed to rural, life seemed to be the characteristic of urbanism. The pessimism of sociology concerning the
pathology of urbanism reflects this focusing on the dislocating
nature of city formation. Louis Wirth's essay "Urbanism as a Way
of Life" was intended as a summary statement for a generation
of research in urban sociology.[1] Its stress is on heterogeneity,
impersonality, destruction of basic social forms, including the
family, and dehumanization through mechanization of social controls. His statement makes sense when we realize that he was
observing transplanted peasants and recording the social behavior
of an immigrant population.

It is not surprising that sociologists since Wirth have piled up
many studies asserting he was wrong.[2] For example, the family
and kinship groups have not disappeared in cities, neighboring
does go on, and anomy is not the pervasive condition. The statements of Durkheim, Simmel, and Wirth might properly be
applied to the national cultures which are undergoing modernization, rather than to urban life as such. If there is an enduring
urban process, it should not simply be associated with urban formation, but also with urban continuation. But, interestingly, once
the United States became a largely industrialized nation, *urban*
ceased to be a useful subcategory of sociology. Urban and rural
ceased to distinguish between forms of social organization. The
folk-urban continuum could not characterize rural-urban differences as agriculture became industrialized and the isolation of
remote places was ameliorated electronically. The abandonment
of urban as a subfield makes sense for a discipline which is observing a completely urbanized nation. At least this view is understandable in sociology of knowledge terms, but ironically it has
led to the abandonment of a specific focus on the urban process
in a nation where this is the most characteristic and pervasive
social process.

The central problem with the Wirth conception of urbanism is
that it confuses urbanism and industrialization. It is true that in

[1] *American Journal of Sociology* 44 (July 1938), pp. 1–24.
[2] Scott Greer, *The Emerging City* (1962), summarized these "revisionist"
statements. See in particular pp. 89ff.

the last two centuries, industrialization has led to city formation, and in the next chapter we will explore the technological basis of this association. But cities existed long before there was industrialization, and this suggests that if we wish to use a concept called *urbanism,* which includes the social processes exemplified by ancient Rome as well as New York, we had better disentangle the concept from industrialization.

Industrialization requires different role structures than preindustrial economic forms. The nineteenth and twentieth centuries furnish many national examples in which the manpower required for industrialization was drawn from communities which had simpler or different role structures. Thus, industrialization required a new organization of society and, in the process of creating it, put several generations through severe dislocating experiences. The social pathologies identified by Wirth and others may well be the attributes of the transition generations.[3] A mature urban population may exhibit a behavior pattern different from this transitional one.

City building preceded industrialization, and it must be viewed as a distinct social process; or industrialization may be seen as a variable which may explain one particular urban form. Because there are such a variety of forms, one cannot treat urbanism as a subculture with particular norms and values. It is preferable to see urbanism as one of man's principal social inventions analogous to bureaucracies and markets. Each of these can be understood as complex forms of organization, which have proved useful for realizing a variety of goals or values.

Urbanism as an Indicator

While the spatial approach to urbanism is embraced by this volume, many of the spatial conceptions of urbanism which have been employed elsewhere are more analytically confusing than the way-of-life approach. Spatial conceptions are most commonly used in aggregate political studies, where urbanism is treated as

---

[3] Charles Tilly states that rapid urbanization is so socially disruptive that such transitional populations have difficulty organizing even collective violence. See his paper delivered at the 1968 American Political Science Association annual meeting, "Urbanization and Protest in Western Europe," p. 7.

4
Metropolitan Political Analysis

an explanatory variable. For example, Seymour Lipset asserts that
the degree of urbanization is related to the existence of democracy.[4] Robert Alford has linked urbanization to the level of class
of those voting.[5] In comparative studies of a number of American
states, urbanization has been used as a correlate of the outcome of
state policy variations;[6] and in voting studies, urbanization is a
commonplace variable.[7] In most of these studies, the operational
definition of urbanization is either the proportion of population in
incorporated places, such as municipalities, or density of persons
per unit of land area. Here, urbanization is used simply as an
indicator, and the specific behavior which is believed to be the
contributor to variations of the dependent variable is far from
clear. For instance, it suggests that persons in high density places
interact differently from those in sparsely populated areas and,
furthermore, that this is a continuous variable.

Urbanization would appear to be synonymous with modernization in Lipset's usage. Urbanization in this sense is an indicator
of a whole set of role and value shifts which take place as societies move from traditional to modern. Just because there are
preindustrial cities, the use of agglomerations as an indicator for
modernization is certainly questionable and misleading. If Gideon
Sjoberg's conclusions can be accepted, industrial and preindustrial
cities may have similar densities, but highly different social
structures.[8]

Urbanization is also used as a variable in explaining internal
differences within modernized societies, such as in the comparative studies of American states. Here, urbanization is clearly *not*

[4] *Political Man* (1960).
[5] *Party and Society* (1963).
[6] Thomas Dye, *Politics, Economics and the Public* (1966); Thomas Cass-
tevens and Charles Press, "The Content of Democratic Competition in
American States," *American Journal of Sociology* 68 (March 1963), pp. 535–
543; Richard E. Dawson and James A. Robinson, "Inter-Party Conjection,
Economic Variables and Welfare Parties in the American States," *Journal of
Politics* 25 (May 1963), pp. 265–289.
[7] Philip Cutright, "Urbanization and Competitive Party Politics," *Journal
of Politics* 25 (August 1963), pp. 552–564; Heinz Eulau, "The Ecological
Basis of Party Systems: The Case of Ohio," *Midwest Journal of Political
Scientists* 1 (August 1957), pp. 125–135; David Gold and John Schmid-
hauser, "Urbanization and Party Competition: the Case of Iowa," *Midwest
Journal of Political Scientists* 4 (February 1960), pp. 62–75.
[8] *The Preindustrial City: Past and Present* (1960).

a synonym for modernization, for no one implies South Dakota is less modern than Massachusetts. Variations in opinions or socialization patterns are often attributed to degree of urbanization, which is often measured by percentage of population in large cities. All of these studies only raise the further question of what population attribute or interaction pattern associated with the urbanization measure underlies its predictive power. Certainly whatever it is, it is not the same thing in such divergent studies as Lipset's, Alford's, and Dye's.

It could be that the reason urbanization works so well as an indicator in a particular setting is that it simply dichotomizes the population. Sometimes this dichotomy reflects occupational clusters with different interests. It may also reflect a division between homogeneous and heterogeneous social areas. It can indicate different positions on a communication network, or it can reflect distinctive political cultures. We really don't know what the indicator *urban* is picking up when these arbitrary spatial measures are used.

Politics and Urbanism

Eclecticism in the use of the term *urbanism* in political science presents an even more serious problem than that posed by the aggregate analysis studies. Urbanism is usually not even a concept in much that passes for urban political studies. *Urban* is a catch-all adjective loosely used to classify a bloc of heterogeneous studies that have little or no theoretical affinity. Urban political studies are not even united by a common set of observable phenomena, let alone interrelationships among propositions. Ostensibly there is a common subject matter, namely, "political events in cities"; but therein lies the problem. The various orientations of urban political studies in the recent past include the following: First there is the orientation toward parties, as was stressed in the "boss rule" studies of the first four or five decades of this century. Here, the primary concerns were with an institution, the *political party,* and the city machine provided an interesting example. A second orientation is toward *legal structures* called municipalities. The field of local government has endeavored to evaluate the influence of formal structures on political outcomes. Concern with this subject dates from the municipal reform movement and continue today, not only among those who study municipal governments, but also among citizen organizations generally. A third orientation is toward *informal power structures*. In many ways, this orientation picked up where the boss rule studies left off. The passing of the old elites as a result of New Deal national legislation and the centralization of American corporate structures resulted in a series of disengagements from local politics by various interests. National laws on labor relations, welfare, and taxation meant that local police were less likely to be used as strike breakers; political machines could make less use of welfare to manipulate voting; and the local property tax was disengaged from local welfare payments. The post–World War II community power structure studies have tried to identify the new local elites which have emerged since these national changes. The intellectual thrust, however, has been in clarifying such general political concepts as power and influence, not urbanism or urban politics.

Still an additional orientation focuses on particular policy areas. There are works on transportation, housing, courts, police, urban renewal, fluoridation, and education. Thus, the orientations among political scientists toward urban politics involve a variety of structures, processes, and policy areas commonly found in cities. While there is nothing intrinsically wrong with these approaches, there is a problem in putting them all together. Moreover, there is nothing that is explicitly urban about any of them. Generally, these studies rely upon proper name identification as a substitute for this shortcoming. We have studies of the government of Chicago, of the parties in Chicago, of power arrangements in Chicago, and of the politics of various policy areas in Chicago. All this tells us is that the researcher has limited his data acquisition to a geographic space commonly designated as Chicago. Since we all know that Chicago is an urban place, there is no further need for defining urban. The implicit assumption of urban studies treated in this fashion is that all these phenomena must be related because they modify a familiar proper noun— Chicago.

In addition to the problem of identifying the linkage among the various sets of observations presumed to explain urban politics, there is also the difficulty of separating urban from nonurban politics. Is everything a city dweller does of a politically relevant nature to be termed urban politics? If that is the case, urban politics loses practically all distinctiveness in advanced industrial nations. We may want to proceed in that fashion, but let the decision be explicit. Some power structure studies come close to this view. The local community is used as a conveniently small laboratory for studying general political phenomena, but the city is not merely a political microcosm of the nation state.

The Local Political Community Studies

A problem with most studies of "local" politics is the lack of clarity about the universe being observed. Some of the arguments between the *pluralists* and *elitists* in the Dahl–Hunter controversy, for example, really grew out of this ambiguity. The debate centered on the definition, measurement, and identification of power, a legitimate and useful exploration. However, another cause of divergence in observations was given less emphasis in those discussions. Little heed was ever given to defining the area, scope of activities, or range of interactions which were to be included in a local political community.

If statements are to be made about a community's power structure, this presumes that there is a definable community. When a person decides to study a political community, he must also decide what should and should not be included; if different studies define the local political system or local political community in quite different terms, inevitably scholars will engage in a lot of talking past one another. For example, if in two studies, both designed to test for pluralism, one equates the local political community with formal local government and the other includes also the policies and decisions of quasi-public civic associations, then the findings are noncomparable. Some political scientists make the distinction between governmental and nongovernmental decisions, using all matters relating to formal local government to define the boundaries of local politics. Others try to identify incidents of conflict resolution. Still others see politics as pervasive throughout all phases of community life. Many researchers have dodged the boundary issue by selecting communities which are well articulated in a spatial sense; that is, they chose cities which are physically isolated from other centers. Actually, however, this practical solution to boundary definition merely obscures the conceptual problem. The choice of isolated communities gives the impression that there are no boundary difficulties. In addition, the spatially isolated single community or settlement is of declining importance in all industrialized nations. The issue may be further sharpened by reviewing how the criteria for defining the local political universe has varied among some of the more prominent case studies.

Hunter, who started the case study sequence of the fifties, paid less attention to government than any subsequent author.[9] But, interestingly, he conceived of Atlanta in terms of the metropolitan region, not the legal city. While the boundaries of the local community were never specified, the unarticulated premise seems to have been that the local community was equated with the economic metropolis. Regional City was roughly the structures, personnel, and supporting social services emanating from a set of spatially proximate economic enterprises. This territorial domain was searched for examples of men exerting power. The local political community was an aggregation of these examples. In passing, Hunter discovered the national impact on the local economy, and thus the dependence of Regional City on forces beyond its boundaries was very real. Consequently, local boundaries were viewed as arbitrary lines across a power network which was ultimately national.

This orientation led subsequent critics to state that Hunter was simply studying one component of the community—the business community.[10] The critics' implication was that although the business community or economic community could be treated as a system which might have impact on other systems (such as welfare and philanthropy), there were other politically salient areas of community life which remained unaffected by them.

Dahl confined his treatment of local politics to decisions of formal political institutions, such as municipal governments, school boards, redevelopment authorities, and political parties.[11]

---

[9] Floyd Hunter, *Community Power Structure* (1962).
[10] Herbert Kaufman and Victor Jones, "The Mystery of Power," *Public Administration Review* 4 (Summer 1954), pp. 205–212.
[11] Robert A. Dahl, *Who Governs?* (1961).

Other behavior is relevant to the extent that it influences the decisions of such bodies. His domain of inquiry was even further restricted by the decision to confine his observations to formal institutions in the city of New Haven, even though many of the interested parties observed were metropolitan citizens. In contrast to Dahl, Vidich and Bensman employed an anthropological approach, which made virtually all behavior in the community politically relevant.[12] Their study of Springdale is not simply a political study, but they speak of the pervasiveness of politics. The two studies stand in marked contrast as to what behavior is considered politically relevant. What Dahl calls slack in the political system and a choice by *homo civitus* to eschew political involvement is often seen by Vidich and Bensman as a form of psychological misrepresentation of reality in those unable to formulate courses of action for reclaiming unfulfilled promises of society. Dahl speaks of unused opportunities to participate, and Vidich and Bensman speak of the structures which frustrate participation.

Some case studies focus on local conflicts and their outcomes, but this strategy requires one to develop criteria for selecting the proper universe of decisions. One response to this problem has been to establish a hierarchy of importance among local decisions or issues. The two criteria commonly used are scope of impact and public opinion. The scope-of-impact criterion posits that a decision affecting the lives of more people is more important than one affecting fewer. This was Dahl's solution, which led him to selection of schools, urban renewal, and political nomination as the focus of inquiry in New Haven.[13] The "public-opinion" criterion involves asking citizens to make judgments about the importance of events. This is essentially the Presthus solution.[14]

The problem with both of these solutions is that neither relates to a conceptually stable universe. In the latter case, the universe of local politics is a function of what each local population says it is. In both, the universe is defined by what conflicts

---

[12] Arthur Vidich and Joseph Bensman, *Small Town in a Mass Society* (1958).

[13] Dahl, *op. cit.*

[14] Robert Presthus, *Men at the Top* (1964).

are generated by existing structures. Only well-developed policy areas, not long-neglected ones, become the basis for analysis. Institutionalized, stable allocations are ignored, and conflict is stressed. However, conflict may not even involve value differences, but may simply be a scramble among the well-situated for a little more. These considerations are at the heart of the criticism of Bachrach and Baratz in their nondecision essay.[15]

Agger, Goldrich, and Swanson propose a solution to the boundary problem, which has some merit.[16] They argue that whenever our society seeks a political solution to social problems, it inevitably changes the scope of government. Thus, scope of government becomes a kind of monitoring device which meters all successful political action. However, as scope changes do not reflect political failures, Agger et al. also include *attempts* to change the scope of government as political events.

Although Agger et al. developed this notion while studying local political communities, it is not a special property of local politics, urban politics, or community politics. Agger et al. are essentially laying out a general strategy for monitoring changes in political systems. In their case studies, they observe territorially contained decision situations which have promise of, or do succeed in, changing the scope of government. The government most affected by actors, so territorially circumscribed, tends to be the local one. Thus, the focus on local government is merely a function of their territorial strategy.

In many respects, the Agger solution is an attractive strategy for comparative research. However, it is not concerned with characterizing a distinctly urban or local process. It is a design which could be employed to study any geographic domain. One could impose a grid on a national population and deal with political events in randomly selected squares. However, such a strategy would be plagued with the problem of dealing with cross boundary interactions, which are considerable in volume and sig-

[15] Peter Bachrach and Morton S. Baratz, "Decisions and Nondecisions: An Analytical Framework," *American Political Science Review* 57 (September 1963), pp. 632–642.

[16] Robert Agger, Daniel Goldrich, and Bert Swanson, *The Rulers and the Ruled* (1964).

nificance. If, indeed, Agger wants to be inclusive about some subset of the national political system, he cannot avoid the notion of a conceptually bounded community anymore than his predecessors could.

Unless we can define urban politics, comparative urban analysis is nearly futile. The foregoing should indicate that community studies, while generally associated with urban studies, completely ignore this problem of establishing a conceptually stable universe of inquiry. Equating urban studies with policy topics, such as police, education, or housing politics, will not do. At one time in our history, there was a legal doctrine of inherently local functions. Even the courts dismissed this bit of transcendental nonsense in the 1930s. Such notions have no place in social science. Another ad hoc solution has been to look at local government as the definer. However, there are some obvious problems in defining urban politics by what local governments do, even for U.S. studies. In the first place, local governments do very different things, and many of the variations are not so much a function of local choice as of state or national law. For a variety of reasons, the distribution of responsibility among levels of government varies from state to state; variations among nations are even greater. Explanations of variations in American local governmental outcomes inevitably pick up this legal noise as a variable when multiple regressions are computed.

Equating local politics with urban politics simply does not resolve the focus-of-inquiry problem. Many that pass for local political studies are really studies of socialization, participation, decision making, conflict resolution, integration, and a variety of other legitimate subjects for political scientists to study. All these areas are part of any political system, including an urban one. However, because of the obscurity with which urbanism is treated, their contribution to urban studies is limited. Indeed, what they have in common is sufficiently obscure to raise questions about whether these "local" studies should even be classified together within social science literature.

It is obvious that there is conceptual confusion concerning urbanism, particularly in political science. The next section suggests a way out.

Urbanism as a Locational Concept

One of the most basic and primitive means that man uses to satisfy his needs and desires is the occupancy of place. The control of place in time is used as a means of access to objects. The unique spot or place which each of us occupies in time defines that to which we can relate around us. Because objects are not randomly distributed, neither is the value and meaning of places. Selective control of place, therefore, becomes an instrument for the attainment of goals. Once man gives *social* meaning to place, the urban process may be said to have begun. Once social structures and processes are created for allocating such places, urban politics may be said to have begun.

In the literal sense, all events take place in time and space. However, all social interactions are not dependent on particular locations. Similarly, all control of location is not, strictly speaking, for the purpose of facilitating interactions. These two distinctions must be further clarified in order to show how the locational approach distinguishes urban from nonurban processes.

But first, one intermediate clarification is essential. The use of the term *access* rather than *interaction,* is deliberate. Many social structures are oriented toward assuring the availability of a value, not only its realization. Urbanism is here defined as an instrument for facilitating human interaction, but the behavior to be included must encompass certain antecedent acts. The concept *access* as used here refers to these efforts to assure the availability of interaction, as well as to interactions themselves.

Returning to the two clarifying statements: First it is recognized that of the totality of social accessibilities, only a subset of these is dependent upon location. Access is dependent upon other social arrangements, such as family, status, group membership, clique, and many other structures. People of the same family usually have access to one another, wherever they are, and it is unlikely that location is a factor. People of the same status may generally have access to one another, but access to specific individuals may depend on space. When an individual wishes to become accessible to many more people, particularly on a continuing basis, location becomes critical. When large numbers of people want to have access to many others with diverse roles, locational strategies are essential. This simple set of considerations lies at the heart of all city and settlement formations.

On the other hand, all efforts to control location are not necessarily to facilitate social access. Control of land for agriculture and farming or for a commanding topographical site for military use may not be initially intended for controlling access. However, subsequent to the occupation of sites or locations for such purposes, it is highly likely that the need for urban strategies and considerations will soon emerge. Mines need artisans, farmers need suppliers, and forts attract camp followers. Each group, in turn, needs to develop relations with others; thus, the nascent state for urban formation is created.

The concept social access, as employed here, is very inclusive, designed to embrace the preconditions for all human interactions, including exchanges of messages and of objects. Access is also presumed to include both positive and negative connotations; that is, location is used to prevent, as well as to facilitate, access. Specific forms of urbanization have devised varying ways of controlling social access, and the messages or exchanges which have been facilitated or limited vary across time and space. Cities serve as religious, military, administrative, commercial, and industrial centers, or as combinations of these. Whether or not these comprise analytically useful subtypes of urbanization is a matter which can be answered only in relationship to particular questions.

The location notion asserts that urbanism is merely an organization of space which facilitates a greater degree of interaction than when spatial considerations are ignored. Such organization is undertaken for a great variety of purposes. When a person moves to a city, he has greater access to more objects than he would outside the city. If the objects of access are limited in number, the precise location is of no great significance. However, if the objects are extremely numerous, the locational decision is salient. It follows that location is a more important precondition for social access in a large city than in a small town.

This notion really lies at the heart of our use of a rural-urban difference; but because of our conceptual ambiguity with terms like urban and rural, we continually muddy the matter. In the absence of a social definition, "rural" is often translated into "farm occupation." The presumption is made that what makes rural areas noncity is the primary occupation. It is not unusual to see urban defined in terms of nonfarm occupations. However, there really is little in the actual content of tilling the soil that is sociologically interesting. The behavior of the modern industrial farmer is probably more akin to many urban occupational groups than to small isolated family farms. The spatial approach clears up this problem. In sparsely populated areas, one cannot manipulate social access patterns by controlling place or space; at least, such control mechanisms have very minimum saliency. By contrast, in the large city, location becomes all important as an instrument of social access.

Similarly, this locational conception overcomes the difficulties of the way-of-life approach, and at the same time incorporates its central insights about role structure. It is certainly true historically that only a locational strategy could weld a very complex role structure. However, there are both ancient and modern examples of massive population aggregations of great density, in which the industrial complex role relationships do not emerge. Are we to consider Bombay nonurban just because the predicted role structures do not occur? Here, and in other places, the village culture has been transported nearly intact from country to city. As sociologist Sjoberg has pointed out, the preindustrial city has a very rigid role structure.[17] Instead of variety, anonymity, and mobility, there is rigidity and class identification. The inhabitant of the industrial city engages in a set of role interactions within the context of many different structures. The preindustrial citizen carries his class identity like a brand, regardless of the role he is performing, and class, not role, has the pervasive influence on the nature of interactions. Whether Sjoberg's generalizations hold or not is beside the point, for, in any case, the role approach is seen as a historically specific rather than a general approach to urbanism.

[17] *Op. cit.*

Historic Urban Forms

If urbanism is viewed as the use of location for social access, the pattern of relationships may be termed the urban form. Every settlement, city, or urban region has a form in that certain activities habitually occupy certain locations. The particular spatial configuration or urban form of a given space at a given time can be largely understood in terms of technology, the objectives of access (values), and the distribution of social and political power. Technology supplies outer limits to what man can do, but the urban form is not simply a technologically determined pattern. Values and power distributions have their own logic and require their own access patterns. In fact, sometimes urban forms are created because of values and power demands which, in fact, exceed the technological capacity of man to accommodate. The results may be traffic jams, wasted human energy, disillusionment, or mass deaths.

Historically, form, values, power, and technology may be treated as associated variables, with the former usually being treated as the dependent variable in urban analysis. Because form becomes translated in cities into rather durable artifacts which have symbolic meanings and technological functions, it becomes a variable which influences the distribution of access. The pattern of access at one particular point in time may influence the pattern of access at a subsequent point in time quite independently of values, power distribution, and technology. The objective of urban analysis is to untangle this web. The examples which follow describe, rather than untangle.

The *sine qua non* for the invention of urbanism as a social device is a technology which can produce some excess in food supplies, some social system which can extract the excess from the producers and distribute it to nonproducers and, finally, some incentive for exploiting the opportunity afforded by these conditions. Certain river valley and tropical natural environments probably first created these circumstances. Given this situation, a limited amount of human inventiveness could greatly improve food production. The possibility of urban formation was thereby provided.

Much that we know about ancient cities is derived from artifacts, and one characteristic artifact, at the heart of the ancient city, was the citadel. Here was the place where the important messages were exchanged. These earliest messages were probably religious in nature, and access to the temple-citadel meant access to the mysteries kept there. Given the existence of a theocracy, the value orientation for social access is established. If rendering the unpredictable understandable involves dealing with the spirits domiciled in a temple, then access to the priests, to the priesthood, and to the priestly knowledge transmitted only in the citadel are major factors structuring life in the theocratic city. Priestly knowledge equaled political power, which was awesome in its completeness, as the pyramids silently testify. Thus, the simple urban form of the guarded temple can be related to the theocratic-authoritarian culture of ancient Egypt.

The citadel has taken many forms, as cultures have valued different messages. When politics and government became the dominant function of the city, the citadel became the palace or great hall, built on an imposing scale and surrounded by obstacles which made it accessible only to those with proper credentials. Churches, forts, and stock exchanges have all been citadels in various times and urban places. If the United States has a citadel, it may well be Wall Street. Access to the money market, and the secrets which make for success there, rivet the attention of the financial world to that small space on Manhattan Island. The increasing densities and the fantastic daily assemblage of people there testify to the importance of access to that citadel's mysteries.

By fitting contrast to others, the early democratic Greeks made their citadel an open space, accessible to all citizens. Furthermore, if legal equality of citizenship is recognized and public affairs are settled through broadly based interaction, if entertainments, meals, and even exercise are communal affairs, then the maintenance of citizen access to these various centers of urban life requires a relatively small-scaled city. Thus, the Greeks maintained a social policy of colonization for taking care of excess population, a policy which was essential for the preservation of equal access by all citizens of the city. If the Greek cities had been allowed simply to grow, like Persian cities, then their social and public institutions would have collapsed. The citadel would have been overrun and rendered dysfunctional. Public discussion can hardly take place in a city of tens of thousands; communication overload occurs as the combination of required message exchanges increases geometrically. Large preindustrial cities have to be politically authoritarian. Thus, the decision on how to handle urban population increases is itself an access policy.

Throughout history, every urbanizing culture has faced the problem of accommodating urban growth. The way this problem is handled influences the resulting interaction pattern. Large urban systems create the possibility of greater and greater combinations of interaction, and the number of combinations increases geometrically with increasing size. Scale changes have consequences for the entire system. In antiquity, large cities generated difficulties for sheer survival because scale and sanitation were linked. Large-scale cities breed high-density nodes as people try to overcome congestion by shortening trips. Historically, this meant that the dead and the night soil could no longer be planted in the gardens: there no longer were gardens, for they were built over as people crowded into the center. Filth clogged the streets, and potable water became scarce. Large urban scale requires proper technology, or there are real problems for survival. As we know today, technological solutions in turn create further problems for technology, air and water pollution being notable examples. Thus, what began as a population move to increase access by agglomeration has sometimes shortened lives; people have literally killed themselves trying to gain access to one another.

The problem of small cities is that they have limits for diversification of products, talents, and variety of interactions. Small cities are highly dependent on external relations for the achievement of many satisfactions. To solve this problem, the Greeks formed a network of colonies around the Mediterranean littoral. Through city specialization and intensive trade, the total range of accessible values and goods was more expansive than any small city could supply alone. This same strategy for increasing total access through planned city specialization again found expression in the Garden City movement of the late nineteenth century.

In fact, however, urban growth is rarely handled through planned colonization (such as the Garden City proposal), but rather through conurbanization, or simply through outward growth. This has been the way of ancient Persepolis, Rome, and New York City. Large cities contain great diversity and extreme specialization. The total range of available goods, services, titillations, and excitements is large indeed, and the competition for gaining access to them is proportionately keen. The accessibility in general depends upon very complex facility structures, and complexity has its own allocating effects; New York, for example, is difficult to enjoy or exploit by the less affluent.

Artifacts are expressions of the structuring of urban access, but as they are relatively permanent, they tend to remain after the reason for their creation has disappeared. Most city dwellers live among physical surroundings which were created for a set of access requirements of a previous generation, even of a previous century. The need for urban renewal, in the sense of a need for recasting the physical form, is a very old problem. When the Greek democracy waned and the Hellenistic polity succeeded, Greek cities began to grow. Small scale was no longer essential, for the political arena was less public. In addition, the cluttered terrain, diminutive streets, and slow-paced, pedestrian-organized space became an impossible artifact environment for the new rulers, who employed great displays of military might and grandeur as means of political control. They needed promenades, so they gouged them through the old terrain. In order for the populace to be properly impressed with ruling power, it had to be accessible to the displays of the ruling class. Nearly two thousand years later, the circuitous and congested street pattern of the medieval city was similarly straightened out by the new Renaissance rulers, when they moved their retinues from the country manor houses to the crowded towns of Southern Europe. For a cast of thousands, you need a big stage. Similarly, Haussmann's boulevard building in Paris improved the accessibility of the police to the multitude. Robert Moses' bridges and highways in New York allowed the Manhattan hub to be more accessible to the New York City hinterland on a daily basis. All great physical renewal projects are attempts to rearrange the pattern of access.

The great boulevards of the Hellenistic city, as well as later major physical barriers, also served to zone the cities into social groupings. Specifying the place of residence of social groups is one of the simplest ways for a political authority to control access. If, in addition, dress is standardized, populations carry their identities on their backs, and the monitoring of access to special areas of the city can be easily administered. The ghetto and the black belt are more recent manifestations of socially sanctioned residential restrictions placed on a visible minority group. The medieval cities used prescribed dress and manners to identify urban population groups, which facilitated keeping people in their place, but because of this spatial zoning dress was less essential for status control. Today's industrial cities are more apt to return to residential zoning as a means of controlling access.

The manipulation of population distributions through space is the most commonplace urban means of allocating access. Whether this is done by an authoritarian caste system, supported by taboos and other mores, or by the operation of an economic market, the result, in terms of the urban process, is socially equivalent. The first objective for contemporary urban political analysis is to identify the control mechanisms which manipulate space and place for the allocation of social access. These are the power structures of urbanism.

Ecology and the Urban Process

The issue may be fairly raised that what is being set forth here is simply a restatement of ecological concerns. Ecology has traditionally focused on the study of man and his environment, including the question of spatial distribution. There is no doubt about the strong intellectual debt my approach to urban analysis owes to ecology. If some want to call this formulation political ecology, so be it. However, several distinctions need to be made between urbanism as conceived here and the way it is used in ecological studies.[18]

Classical ecology attempted to explain human territorial or-

---

[18] For a review of development in ecological theory see George A. Theodorson (ed.), *Studies in Human Ecology* (1961), introductory pages; and Sidney Willhelm, *Urban Zoning and Land Use Theory* (1962), chaps. 2, 3.

ganization through biotic rather than cultural variables. The organization and distribution of man in a territory was viewed as a function of such noncultural factors as energy supplies, population pressures on food supply, and technology. This classical view was abandoned because the distinction between social and biotic proved untenable. Specific studies of population configurations invariably had to introduce variables derived from social structures or extant values.

The biotic-cultural distinction has disappeared from explicit statements in ecology, but schools of thought derived from these sources continue. The neoclassicists (materialists) continue to focus on a given population as their unit of analysis and to analyze the relationship of population composition to technology, physical habitat, and social organization. The voluntarists—or those stressing a cultural approach, who may consider Milla Alihan, Warner Gettys, and Walter Firey as their progenitors—focus on the individual as the unit of analysis and explain certain spatial configurations in terms of individual value preferences. The materialists stress forms of economic competition as contributors to spatial distribution, while the culturalists stress shared symbols and values as the sources of explanatory variables.[19]

The members of these two schools of thought are often loath to wear these labels, and their empirical work is not so neatly categorized. Indeed, there is a point at which such classification is a barren exercise, because the real issue is the capacity of each approach to explain what it specifies it can. As it reaches the issues of free will and determinism or psychological reductionism, the discussion teeters on the brink of an age-old quagmire of philosophy.

The basic insight of ecology of both schools is that the investigation of territorial organization of man involves special analytical problems that differ from explanations pertaining to other forms of social organization. The spatial configuration of human populations is obviously not random. At the same time it is far from clear that a spatial configuration, even when identified as a community, can be treated as a social system. While most social organizations can be disaggregated into role and role relation-

[19] Willhelm, *op. cit.*, p. 32.

ships, the treatment of the urban community, or spatially defined populations, in this language inevitably involves difficulty. While some spatially defined populations may be socially organized or structured, this may be only fortuitous. This fact lies at the heart of the problem which divides human ecologists into the two historic camps. The early materialists, realizing they were dealing with a special type of social configuration, attempted to explain community structure and patterns in subsocial terms. Urban communities seemed to be formed by unseen and unidentified forces. The notion of subsociality was an unfortunate one, but it really was an effort to state that something different was taking place here. Man could not be studied solely in terms of the social units about which he was aware; there was more to city form than composite social structures. The volunteerists, or cultural ecologists, resolve the problem by treating the spatial distributions as the result of individual value preferences and strategies. This is all right as far as it goes, but it renders urban behavior analogous to all other behavior. If that is the case the only thing that distinguishes ecology from sociology is the phenomenon being studied and ecological processes are not different from any other social processes.

This volume operates more in the tradition of the neomaterialists (the name is misleading), which asserts that a distinct mode of analysis is needed for explaining spatially defined social aggregates. This route rejects the notion that urbanism should be equated to, or placed as a subcategory of, communal social life. Community usually is associated with some kind of self-consciousness among its membership, or with a social structure which defines the relationship among the members, or with both. Whether these are attributes of all urban forms is something to be demonstrated, not assumed.

Until the present, there has been little interest shown by political scientists in this controversy within ecology or in ecology in general. Political ecology has usually been used as a synonym for geopolitics. Inquiry is limited to the relationship between natural barriers, resources, geographic positions of military significance, and other factors which might relate to international relations. Political science has only recently begun to penetrate ecology as an approach to subnational or urban analysis. To complete this chapter, the connection between the definition of urbanism presented, the concerns of ecology, and the questions that should be posed in urban politics will be demonstrated.

Urban locations involve social access patterns, which are often of a very complex nature, and the rewards and incentives systems for constructing these linkages are equally complex. Economic advantage, status, symbolic identification, and physical and psychic comfort are among the possible goals. A given urban form usually satisfies various values to varying degrees. Residual dissatisfactions imply that sociospatial configurations involve competition, as the early ecologists well understood. Urbanism also involves complementary and reciprocal relations, as many urban economists and sociologists have made explicit. Most attempts to elaborate the configurations have focused on market analysis or intergroup relations. We have a picture of place being allocated by the pricing system. We have an image of intergroup frictions among diverse populations and individual responses to opportunities and aspirations leading to certain patterns of population distribution. What is lacking is the allocative political structures which accompany these processes. This lacuna may result from the absence of a political science subfield which focuses on urbanism as a distinct social process.

Chapter 2

TECHNOLOGY,
LOCATION,
AND
ACCESS
STRATEGIES

Introduction

If wealth, status, and power can be considered instrumental resources used in realizing certain other values in life, then location can be conceived the same way. While wealth, status, power, and location are, to a certain degree, interchangeable resources, they are not all equally appropriate for achieving specified ends. All tend to be a general coinage of exchange, but of the four, location is the least liquid and the most specific as to its utility. An understanding of the use of locations in urban life is a first step toward perceiving how the social structures distribute access through control of space. This chapter will give a nontechnical portrait of location as a means to access, of how location is affected by technology, and finally how location is allocated by social structures through the employment of resources.

In Chapter 1 urbanism was conceived in terms of locational strategies and orientations. Initially, let us proceed, through illustration, to examine how these orientations are linked to access requirements. Economic institutions offer the easiest examples, because the goals of such organizations are readily understandable. To say that all firms seek to maximize profits is, in fact, a gross oversimplification, and it flies in the face of much evidence; yet, this notion provides a convenient fiction, which is analytically useful. Let us, therefore, assume that firms seek to improve their access to social groupings or organizations when such access promises to increase profit; that is, they seek access to more or better paying customers, superior supplies, and more satisfactory labor sources. Place or location serves as a means of access to these goals in several ways. As the industrial recruiters and locational analysts are well aware, enterprises evaluate each location in terms of the kind of access it provides. Some industries want access to cheap labor; others, to skilled. The first requires a location on public transportation routes which connect with low-rental areas. The latter requires a location convenient to an automotive network; hence, probably near a freeway linked to suburban residences. Some industries are dependent on external economies; others are not. If the former is the case, the plant may be drawn to the older core, high-density center, which has a complex mix of available short-term rental space, a variety of supplies obtainable on short notice and in small lots, and the requisite combination of skills and services conveniently nearby. The plant which is relatively independent of external economies will seek the cheaper, less congested space on the edges of, or even away from, metropolitan areas.

It would be possible to spin out a long list of considerations relevant to the access requirements of given firms. This is the particular province of those who counsel firms on facility location. The focus here, however, is on general categories of action.

Technology and Access

Generally, in land economics, the concept of space friction is employed to denote the problem of accessibility. Since no two enterprises can occupy the same site, they cannot be accessible to each other on a simultaneous basis. Space friction is often used to characterize the resulting problem. Space friction is a time-distance concept. An expenditure of energy is involved in overcoming either dimension (time or distance). In an era of technological advances in electronic communications, and the building and subsequent congesting of freeways, it is common knowledge that physical distance does not always define the real interactional distance between two points. The cross-town trip in Manhattan is more expensive than a trip to Westchester on some days. A telephone call to Hong Kong may be an easier form of access than climbing a stair.

The access pattern exhibited by an urban complex is the product of many variables. Two of the most powerful shaping forces are energy and technology. The energy available to any society places a limit on what it can do. Technology is the process of cost reduction for performing acts with a given unit of energy. Energy technology refers to the cost reduction in making usable energy available. The raw form in which energy is available and the characteristic of the device employed to convert it to usable forms both affect the dependent social structure.[1] A brief look at the manner in which energy technology has shaped cities will be instructive.

The technology of the nineteenth century necessitated an urban spatial implosion. The peculiarities of coal-energy technology required high densities and produced a dirty by-product, thereby creating a congested and disagreeable city. The steam engine as an energy converter is more efficient when it enables a large surface of water to be exposed to flame. At the same time, steam engines have relatively small energy fields, as power is delivered by mechanical and friction-prone devices, such as wheels and belts. In striving for greater efficiency, nineteenth-century manufacturing entrepreneurs built massive steam converters in order to achieve the proper boiler sizes. While this produced an efficient stationary power source, it had limited utility for powering urban transportation vehicles. A large steam locomotive is a particularly poor power source for intraurban transport of people, for the inertia of large steam engines makes stopping and starting a costly business. Knowing these simple facts about the limits of the nineteenth-century energy technology, we can go a long way towards understanding some of the locational developments that took place.

Manufacturing plants require labor and material inputs. The most profitable plant was one powered by a large steam engine. Large plants required a large labor force and generated much freight hauling, but there was no equally efficient technology for

[1] For many of my insights about energy technology, I am indebted to Fred Cottrell, *Energy and Society* (1955). See his early chapters particularly.

delivering workers to the plant or for the movement of freight over short distance. It was necessary to rely upon low-energy converters; namely, men and horses, to service these needs. This meant workers had to live close to the plant, hence the need for mixed land use or the intermixing of residential and industrial land. Similarly, cities attempted to shorten the low-energy street hauling of freight by increasing densities in industrial areas. Vertical loft buildings, huddled around a steam power source, spewed an unbelievable congestion into the abutting narrow streets. The use of loft factories not only conformed to the belt-limited energy field of the steam engine, but also allowed more plants to crowd near strategic, fixed terminal points of the unwieldy steamboat and locomotive. Docks and railyards had to be brought right into the city in order to shorten local transport lines. Unfortunately, this is where they still remain.

Thus, the nineteenth-century city was one of mixed land uses, high density, and vertical factories. It also exhibited a locational orientation toward docks, railroads, and central areas. In the terms of sociologist MacKenzie, the nineteenth-century city had high dependence on central institutions.[2] Lines of access tended to converge at selected nodes. The heart of the city was truly in the center. (Of course, the whole scene was continuously sprinkled with coal soot; so it was a very dirty place as well. From historical accounts, today's cities would be judged clean by comparison.)

The relationship between location and access was clearly dramatized in the nineteenth-century city. Location of a store on the main street assured access to customers. A location near a railhead assured the cheapest way to overcome space friction in handling freight. Hotels were built near rail depots where, as in the case of New York, buyers stayed. The fashion industry gravitated to the hotel area in order to reach buyers, hence, the origin of the present-day garment district. The fact remains, however, that the factory which locates on a wooded knoll on the outskirts of the metropolis today is engaged in the same locational process. The twentieth-century plant may be seeking cheap land or a resort-like atmosphere for its research employees

[2] Roderick Mackenzie, *The Metropolitan Community* (1933), p. 71.

or simply satisfying the pastoral yearnings of the owner. None of these changes the fact that the locational decision discriminates in favor of increasing access to certain things and reducing it to others. Today's decentralization trend, i.e., the tendency of firms to move to lower density areas, still exemplifies the urban process. Contrary to most historical trends, changes in urbanization may now be characterized by a reduction, rather than by an increase, in density.

Technological constraints were such that the nineteenth-century set of limits resulted in an unbelievably poor human habitat. Twentieth-century technology is less obviously limiting, and consequently the technological variable is less easily related to the emerging urban pattern. However, the impact of present-day technology can be easily seen when we realize that the internal combustion engine, as a converter, operates on opposite principles from the steam engine. The problem is cooling the thing, not making it hotter. As a result, small gasoline engines were more practical than large ones. The small internal combustion solved, in a fashion, the short-haul problem. The high-energy-driven commuter vehicle became possible. It only remained for the perfection of the electric motor to further the miniaturization process and make way for the great industrial dispersal. Electronic communication and computer technology are probably today's foremost agents of change; yet, their full consequences have not been spelled out.

Social Value and Location

Thus far, we have been approaching the subject of access and location by illustration. Let us now make a more definitive statement. All locations occupied by man assume a social meaning, which is derived from the access afforded by occupancy of that location. The notion of access can be further elaborated by focusing on the means by which it is expressed. The social meaning of location is derived from the fact that place facilitates access to (1) artifacts, (2) networks of interactions, and (3) social structures.

1. Artifacts are probably the least interesting source of social meaning for urban places. But buildings and structures *do* have

utilitarian value. Artifacts may also connote symbolic meaning derived from past occupancies or events associated with them. Finally, artifacts orient us physically and visually. Thus, artifacts as such give meaning to a place through their utility, symbolism, and ability to act as obstacles or channels for physical and visual movement.

2. Each site is unique in the physical sense in that it is the only point which has the same relationship to all other sites. To the extent that social interactions or exchanges are based upon propinquity, a location defines a possible network of interactions. Location, pure and simple, is the key to many social exchanges. Even with technologically advanced communication and transportation, we are not freed from space; they have merely transformed the uses of propinquity. Thus, each place or site has advantages for facilitating a certain combination of interactions; hence, location has social meaning in terms of the exchanges which it makes more possible or convenient.

3. Certain social structures are geographically bounded in a formal sense. That is, the rules of the social structures include spatial boundaries. Municipalities, school districts, voluntary agencies, utilities, newspapers, and a variety of other services have boundaries to their operations. These boundaries may be set legally or by the norms of the social organizations. All occupants of the terrain within those boundaries have access, at least potentially, to those structures. Each location has meaning in terms of the many structures which embrace that location within their bounded territory of operation.

Thus, when a family occupies a house, the value of that occupancy is derived from the artifact (house properties), from interactions facilitated (commuting, shopping, social interactions), and from supporting social structures (local government, schools, utilities). The economic market is an important mechanism for allocating sites by assigning site value. However, urban locational allocation is far from equivalent to land economics. Furthermore, though the above description of locational orientations is stated in *choice* terminology, it is still questionable whether individual choice behavior is the proper explanatory basis for urban studies. In any event, the constraints on individual choice are not simply economic.

Allocation of Access

Access conveys the notion of availability rather than of actual use. As used here, it is intended to connote the notion of available social *interactions*. If I have access to my neighbor, I may borrow the proverbial lawnmower, and the door will not be slammed in my face when I ask. The choice of the term *access* rather than *interaction* is deliberate. It is assumed that anticipation of the available, rather than the actual, interactions motivates adjustments in location. Access is the prerequisite for actual interaction and is thus a more inclusive concept than interaction itself. It takes note of the fact that perceptions affect behavior and perceptions of access will influence interaction patterns. The task is to explain the state of access—the map of accessibilities.

Most observers of the city scene comment on its variety. The city is the place where one can choose his style of life. In this sense, there may be a basic complementarity to spatial location in urban areas, rather than competition. The fact that all do not choose to occupy urban space in the same way, or for the same reasons, adds up to richer varieties of experience, combinations of opportunities, and refinements in the texture of living. There is obvious truth to this picture, and if we were interested in poetry rather than politics, we could stop here. Despite the complementary nature of a diverse population, at some point, the access of one becomes blocked by the actions of another. In this basic competitive situation, politics begins.

The rush to the suburbs, crowded highways, ghettoes and slums, decaying empty factories and stores, declining core-city populations, urban renewal, riots, and air pollution are a few of the indicators that the allocation process does not operate to the satisfaction of all and that the distribution has inequities. Because the dissatisfaction is quite obvious and the inequities real, we might expect efforts both to change and to maintain the status quo.

There are essentially two options open for those who wish to employ a location strategy to change their access within the urban complex. They can move or they can change the characteristics of the place they presently occupy. The latter course of action essentially involves bringing others into more accessible positions. Urban locational decisions, indeed, the very creation of cities, are the net product of many people trying to become more accessible to one another. The same process that creates cities continues after they are formed. The larger the urban complex, or the more numerous and specialized the interactions demanded, the more critical becomes the locational decision of each urbanite. In the beginning, when settlements were small, one's physical presence in a settlement created the potentiality of access to all others located there. However, as urban complexes increase in size, and/or the requirements for access become more numerous, mere presence in the settlement is not sufficient to yield satisfactory access; instead, a strategic location within the settlement or city has to be sought.

The two options or strategies are pursued simultaneously in all urban areas. In the United States today most people solve their access problems by moving. Each year, thousands of families change their domiciles, merchants change their locations in hot pursuit of customers, and industries move, looking for cheaper inputs or lowered costs in delivering outputs to customers. However, this process of population shifts is a most complex affair. One can only go where one is allowed to go. The limits are placed not only through the distribution of resources (wealth, information, status, etc.), but also through the fluidity of these resources and through political barriers and facilitating channels. Technology merely supplies outer limits or ground rules which all are bound by. Technology never displaces economics and politics in place manipulation.

Fluidity of resources means the capacity to translate assets into locational control. This includes the capacity to exchange one location for another. Janowitz coined the phrase "community of limited liability"[3] to indicate that most American urban dwellers have very little stake in a given place, that there is little to prevent them from packing up and moving. However, some cannot move and gain any advantage; their access requirements are tied to a specific location. For example, commercial enterprises whose primary asset is personalized services have a problem following their clientele who may disperse to many new

---

[3] Morris Janowitz, *The Community Press in an Urban Setting* (1952).

locations. Merchants who sell goods with objectively defined properties have less trouble moving than those who sell subjectively defined goods. A druggist whose business is primarily dependent upon personal relationships built up over years with customers, including informal medical counseling, has difficulty replicating such an access pattern in a new location. On the other hand, a merchant whose business is keyed to bargain sales of standardized goods should have fewer relocation problems. "Good will," which is neighborhood specific, is a very unliquid asset. Many of the tragedies among small merchants in urban renewal areas result from this fact. The *immobiles* tend to include small merchants, businesses with ethnic clienteles, or those whose "asset" is knowledge of a particular place, such as realtors, neighborhood newspapers, and certain salesmen.

With the exception of these cases of nonfluid resources, those with more resources, generally speaking, are more likely to achieve preferred location than those with fewer. One of the means through which those with large resources solve their locational problems is local area planning. Shopping center complexes, planned neighborhoods, industrial parks, or new towns are all attempts to define the access requirements of a given population in advance and to assemble the proper mix of persons in the proper artifact context. Urban redevelopment is a surgical form of this strategy; here the attempt is made to create a new environment, which will be sustained by satisfying the access requirements of the remaining old urban cells. Needless to say, urban renewal decisions for tearing down are not always guided by an understanding of the social meaning of places. Rubbled blocks which lay fallow for years document this failure.

Resources, such as wealth, information, or status, cannot always be directly translated into location control. Alternatively, structures may be formed which create channels and barriers. These allocating structures may be classified into coalitions and communities.

Collective Urban Political Strategies

Coalitions and communities are both collectivities in which there is joint, coordinated political action by group members. In a *coalition,* members are always free to opt out and achieve goals through individual strategies or by joining other coalitions. Members of a *community* have common destinies, in which the goals of each member are inextricably tied to the goals of the particular collectivity. Thus, a member of a community cannot improve his access by opting out.

The characteristic political structure in the American urban process is the coalition, not the community. As investments in places increase, coalitions augment individual mobility as means of achieving and controlling access. Coalitions are formed to facilitate wanted interactions and prevent unwanted ones. This may take the form of keeping the "wrong" people or businesses out. Among the common urban coalitions are realty boards, bankers associations, chambers of commerce, redevelopment authorities, and suburban municipal governments. They all seek advantages for members through manipulation of access, usually as it pertains to a particular domain.

Barriers can be created and tests of admission can be administered to screen entrances into a domain. A classical legal instrument for this is zoning. Zoning is an explicit political means of abridging economic market allocation of land among various uses. A builder whose structures have relatively high value in relationship to the land parcel can afford to bid more for land than a builder constructing lower value structures, such as single-family dwellings. By preventing an apartment from being built in a single-family dwelling unit section, the short-run price of the intended site is probably depressed. Thus, zoning coalitions are formed to control access patterns directly in the face of contrary pressure from the market. Zoning is the mechanism by which people band together to "keep up the neighborhood." Countering coalitions form to obtain short- or long-run profits by changing the land uses allowed. In most zoned areas, there are complex sets of zoning coalitions arrayed against one another. However, as is often the case, individual members of the coalitions act unilaterally to improve their access, often causing these coalitions to become unstable.

The coalition is not to be confused with an interest group. The access requirements of urbanites tend to be discreet and individual, just as the sites they occupy are unique. For this very reason, terrain-based coalitions tend to have low cohesion. Political groups, organized around shared interests, identified with occupation, religion, economic status, or avocation, are not affected by urban changes. When a family moves from Chicago to Winnetka, it takes along the personal attributes of family members. The Chicago-based locational interests are exchanged, however, for Winnetka's. The family moves away, literally, from one set of urban coalitions into a different set. The type of access desires may be constant, but moving may help undermine the coalition left behind in Chicago and reinforce, or perhaps change, the one joined in Winnetka. Interests based on the characteristics of persons can be aggregated nationally, e.g., interests based on having income from stocks and bonds. Interests based on a specific position of access within an urban complex are hard to aggregate into national political organizations, but they may be even harder to aggregate on a city basis. The competitive nature of urbanism is highlighted in the local context. The gap between national and local labor-union policies on public housing illustrates this fact.

A second urban access allocating social structure is the community, an example of which is the traditional ethnic neighborhood. If the most prized access pattern of an individual Italian immigrant is to be situated so that he has maximum face-to-face contact with a particular set of other Italian immigrants, then a collectivity of such persons would comprise a community. Obviously, no individual member can improve his position by leaving the group. Many ethnic groups formed communities on their arrival, but this was especially characteristic of the Italians. Moreover, the access desired was not to Italian immigrants per se, but to persons from a certain community in Italy. This constitutes a nearly ideal type of community, for here is a set of individuals with a common life destiny which cannot be achieved if the composition of the set is substantially altered. By contrast, many middle-class "communities" do not qualify as communities, according to our use of the concept. If all that is desired is a certain set of amenities and norms, as opposed to interaction with a set of specific individuals, only a coalition is required.

Because it is impossible to aggregate the specific access demands of communities, claims are rarely made on their behalf at higher levels of government.

In its most extreme manifestation, community assumes an antisocial stance vis-à-vis the larger society. The Cosa Nostra, for example, has all the attributes of community. Similarly, nationalism is a form of community disturbing to world peace and order. This sense of community is uncommon in our urban scene. It is a more common attribute of European urban life, where allegiance to a set population has been particularly strong in the past. Although American small-town patriotism provides some evidence of being community-like, most American places, whether urban, rural, or small town, are more like coalitions.

One of the recent interesting manifestations of self-conscious community building is among black radicals. It is one of the few recent examples of an American group asserting that the realization of individual interests is radically dependent on common group achievements. Rejection of integration means the rejection of coalitions and individual adaptive moves as the mode of solving urban political problems for blacks. The black radicals, who advocate some form of separatism or black allegiance, are saying that the only beneficial access for the black individual is through the black community, or that successful access to whites is contingent on a collective redefinition of black-white relations. It is the community characteristic that makes their view truly "radical" in American perspective. It counters the American individualistic way.

The measurement and scaling of behavior which is oriented toward coalition, as opposed to community formation is one of the unfulfilled tasks of urban research. Much of the loose talk about loss of community pride, rootlessness, and nomadism in modern life assumes the meaningfulness of such a scale. However, we do not know much about the conditions under which behavior is most community oriented and most coalition-like.

Recapitulation

Let us recapitulate the foregoing into one formulation. Figure 1 presents the urban process described in this chapter. It is pos-

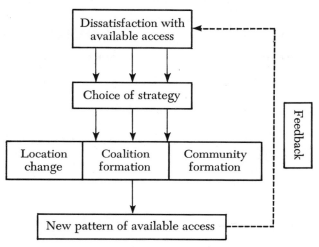

Figure 1. Model of Urban Political Process

sible to formulate this process in systems terms, but all the conditions for a systems approach have not been set forth. The universe of observations which must be undertaken to study the way in which the pattern is reshaped is largely a matter of empirical observation. We don't know if the metropolitan area is one or many systems of access manipulation. However, any investigation which confines itself merely to observations of collective actions (coalitions and community formation) is bound to yield a truncated and warped view of urban change. The fact remains that most urban dwellers vote by moving van, not by ballot box, and that coalitions, not communities, are the characteristic urban collectivity. Coalition stability may be the most important political variable in shaping urban form.

However, in order to describe the urban process it is necessary to clarify what the unit of analysis is. Because it is difficult to describe urban process as the product of individual actions, we must now introduce the concept of the sociospatial unit.

Chapter 3

SOCIOSPATIAL
UNITS
AND
THEIR
COALITIONS

The Unit of Analysis

Urban politics as defined here is a means by which space and place are socially controlled and allocated in order to facilitate or limit accessibility. Access, the necessary precondition for interaction, is inextricably a part of the general process of social interactions. City life is characterized by throngs, crowds, commuters moving, social gatherings, communication wires buzzing with messages, and the formation of nodes where interactions are occurring on various levels of intensity. If we could represent the people of a city as dots on a field and conceive the movements of the dots as interactions, the resulting image would be a complex array of particles moving against one another, forming nodes of various sizes, breaking up, regrouping, and dispersing in an unbelievably intricate pattern. Although this picture is plausible and suggestive of a model, it lacks analytical usefulness for empirical research. One problem is that the particle must be defined.

The most fundamental sociological assumptions warn us against using the individual person as the focal point of analysis, i.e., as the particle; for, alas, man is not free, but operates within the confines of social structures. In urban analysis, it is also necessary to heed this fact. The urban process is clearly not a random-interaction pattern among individuals; nor is it the result of the actions of myriad self-willed and calculating individuals.

It is essential to identify the salient urban social structures which underlie the patterns.

But first it is necessary to clarify the use here of *place* and *space*. *Place* and *location* will be used much as locational theorists use *site;* that is, a place or site is a point which has a unique set of relationships to all other points. As a sheer abstract geographic spatial notion, this is a precise term. *Space* refers to the relationship among places. One place is spatially close to or far from another, depending upon the accessibility of one place to another. In a social context, linear distance does not measure access, or even the cost of access. Barriers of a technological, social, physical, or political nature may act as impediments. Thus, the notion of a unique place must be abandoned in urban analysis. There may be a variety of places which offer equal opportunities for a given set of interactions to occur. This does not destroy the notion, however, that places can be viewed hierarchically, offering greater or fewer opportunities for access to specified other places. Thus, place as a commodity has attributes which fix it somewhere between the unique site of the geographer and a standardized product which can be replicated in large volume. Many places, including most of the socially remote spots on the globe, are practically useless as means of social access. Some, though, are uniquely situated, and these generally are in urban centers.

Let us consider the urban scene initially as a set of socially desirable places within a physical space that has proximate boundaries. This is a way of characterizing conventional, modern cities. A city may be observed to be covered with physical structures. These physical artifacts, from a social scientist's point of view, are like so many shells inhabited by social units. Just as shell characteristics have some functional relationship to the contained biological organism, so do buildings to the social structures which inhabit them. These basic social units of the urban scene will be called *sociospatial*. Such units have the common characteristics of achieving unit goals through establishing access to other systems, in part, by choice of place in space. The urban process may be described in terms of the pattern of relationships which emerge among the sociospatial units.

The systems concept can be applied to describe these basic social units. Each unit comprises a set of roles. Interaction among role occupants leads to collective decisions by the sociospatial units on locational strategies for affecting interactions with other units. In brief, the basic social structure, *sociospatial unit,* may be conceived as a social system which employs access strategies based on location. While the norms pertaining to particular roles within a given system may be divergent regarding access requirements, to the extent that a location is essential for the maintenance of the sociospatial unit, the conflicts inherent in these divergent norms must be reconciled and subordinated to a collective decision. Internal conflict within a unit may arise because role occupants in any sociospatial system are also role occupants in other systems. The key to understanding the reciprocal impact of roles on individual behavior is an empirical matter, and the relationship suggests one set of questions to be investigated by urban research.

A few illustrations might prove useful in demonstrating the utility of the concept. One of the most pervasive and commonplace examples of a sociospatial unit is the household. Such a unit must obviously involve itself in a space and place strategy. The role occupants who constitute the family or household members are also generally role occupants in other social systems. The domicile location may well be a function of the needed lines of access, enabling each household member to operate in the variety of social settings he prefers, such as work, school, or church. However, the access requirements of the role occupants of a household are not exhausted by these well-structured, multiple role involvements; access to more casual and less structured social interactions is also important, such as friends, entertainment centers, and club meetings.

One of the questions in urban research is why people move. It is often investigated as an attitude-response type of problem, in which the respondent indicates whether the house, the grass, or the children's schooling was the basis of the change. This same question formulated in terms of role stress might yield more informed answers. Particularly if posed over time or between various cultures, it would indicate the differing hierarchy of access values which change through time and among cultures.

Jobs, kinship, friendship, and cultural claims undoubtedly change over time. The decisional structures within households must also vary. The locational decisions of a child-oriented family should differ from those of a family in which the father's wishes are law.

Early ecological studies attempted to achieve generalizations about urban population movements through developing laws of invasion and succession. Employing the concept of the access-seeking unit may allow an improved formulation. For example, access to ethnic group social structures was one of the important considerations in determining domicile location for immigrant families. As long as a foreign language was used, propinquity to other users of the mother tongue was essential for carrying on daily tasks, as well as for a feeling of social well-being. Some studies suggest that the high value of spatial propinquity to peer members among immigrants may continue for several generations.[1] Others have indicated that propinquity may be a declining necessity, even among populations still heavily influenced by ethnic ties. Parenti suggests that access to fellow ethnic types may be very durable and last for generations, but propinquity as a condition of access may subside.[2] Thus, the disappearance of the invasion-succession phenomena can best be explained by looking at the behavior of households in terms of location-access relationships.

One advantage of employing the sociospatial system as the basic unit of urban analysis is that comparable information can be obtained from what are seemingly heterogeneous entities. All land-occupying systems have the required definitional property. These include factories, stores, churches, lodges, and enterprises of a diverse nature. From the accumulation of the decision rules of the various units, one can begin to construct the pattern of locational orientations. At this point, we probably know the most about the decision rules of profit-making enterprises. The kinds of structured relations between a plant and the elements of its urban

[1] Nathan Glazer and D. Patrick Moynihan, *Beyond the Melting Pot* (1963).
[2] Michael Parenti, "Ethnic Politics and the Persistence of Ethnic Identification," *American Political Science Review*, 61 (September 1967), pp. 717–720.

environment required for a profitable operation can be specified in a fairly accurate fashion in the short run.

Since all interactions literally take place in time or space, do all interacting sets of roles constitute a sociospatial unit? In a literal sense, they do. However, the impact of their behavior on the urban process may be relatively weak and small. Casual and ephemeral interacting sets usually make few claims on the place of activity. Some relatively stable sets interact in a fashion that is nearly independent of place. The floating crap game, the chance encounter, a family reunion, or a negotiating session are place-occupying interactions. However, their impermanence diminishes the possibility of engaging in complementary or competitive locational strategies which will impose any enduring structure on patterns of access. The sociospatial concept endeavors to abstract out the place-relevant behavior of social structures. The more relevant locational considerations are to the goals of the structure, the more likely that the unit will be engaged in urban processes and urban politics. If those considerations are, in addition, relatively permanent, then we have identified an urban interest and a likely source of continuing force in shaping the urban form.

Having established the basic unit of analysis, how do we proceed to build up an explanation of the urban political process? This must be done through both the understanding of the internal decisional processes of units and the interaction patterns among them. Let us first give brief consideration to the former.

The units have been described in systems terms. This means we can disaggregate a unit into roles, role norms, and role occupants. Since a unit must locate by definition, there must be some kind of internal decisional structure for establishing authority. For some units, such as factories or stores, this authority structure is fairly formally established. Workers are unlikely to be participants in many of the authority's decisions, except to the extent that enterprises must treat labor as an input; consequently, satisfactory labor must be accessible to the plant or store location. Families probably have more complex decisional structures. Variance may be attributed to social class, life style, stage of life cycle, ethnicity, and personality.

The outcome of the internal decisional process is not only a function of the internal decision structure, but also of the available resources. Resources include not only wealth, but information and status as well. Of the resource factors, we know the most about wealth. Land economics has endeavored to understand location through rent. We also know something about status in relationship to segregation and other forms of discrimination. The least is known about the way information affects locational behavior. Does the information available to urban actors limit or channel the alternatives which are explored?

Role conflicts for individuals, conflict derived from role differentiation within the sociospatial unit, and resource limitations all place units under stress when they formulate locational strategies. Under certain situations of internal stress, the sociospatial unit breaks up. Frequently role occupants drop out: Families break up, people quit their jobs, businesses decentralize, congregations dwindle, and customers move away and stores fail. However, stress more normally leads to a choice of an adaptive strategy, one which realigns access so that the total access of all role occupants is more satisfactory. The leading strategies are relocation and coalition formation, of which we will now consider the latter.

Urban Coalitions

The access situations of any sociospatial unit can be viewed as more or less satisfactory at any time. When any given unit changes its access position, the overall pattern of access is affected; thus, the urban milieu is potentially a transitory and insecure one. Some stability is preserved, however, simply because mutually rewarding relationships will tend to endure. A successful business, a congenial neighborhood, and a full congregation are all examples of reciprocally satisfying sets of relationships. However, competing values and incompatible access requirements among the various sociospatial units constantly introduce threats into the urban milieu. In order to cope with these uncertainties, units resort to the commonest of political ploys, the formation of coalitions.

The assumption in coalition formation is that increased power can be aggregated through combining the resources of participants who have common or compatible goals. The rewards from coalition formation are the maintenance or enhancement of the access pattern of coalition members through preventing interference from nonmembers. There is a bewildering array of urban coalitions; any classification of them should be guided by some analytical consideration. The descriptive classification used here is ordered by certain classes of objects to which urban coalitions are oriented.

The commonest type of coalition is a security community, organized to protect a domain. Examples of this include street gangs, neighborhood associations, industrial parks, shopping centers, main street associations, and many local governments. The identification of access interests with a particular urban space occurs for several differing reasons.

Propinquity is an easy means of controlling access, and thus spatially homogeneous areas are often formed around certain shared access needs. The residential neighborhood is a case in point. If there is a high value in having one's child associate with other children from homes with roughly comparable child rearing standards, a spatial strategy is the obvious means for achieving this goal. As children tend to live in the immediate environment of the home, the residential neighborhood is very importantly a child's world. (In planning, the whole notion of a neighborhood elementary school was originally predicated on the spatial range which could be handled by a six-year old child, unaided and on foot.) Many factors, of course, are relevant in neighborhood selection. Casual sociality, status identification, outdoor domestic behavior (i.e., attitudes toward Christmas decorations, lawn practices, and barbecue parties), and architectural tastes are among the factors which define the compatibility of close cohabitation of residential space.

The teen-age street gang might be used as a paradigm of the domain or turf-based coalition. Perhaps the spatial neighborhood has more meaning for younger persons than for adults. In fact, we might assume that there is a correlation between age and the spatial size of one's daily world, but with a decline in the curve at the end of life. While very young children have playmates, nothing approximating an urban coalition emerges until approximately the teen-age years. The teen-age gang coalition is the primitive urban political formation. The membership is well defined, the norms of the group quite real, albeit far from explicit, and the boundaries of the turf specific in the minds of the gang members. Gangs follow a variety of strategies, which approximate the practices of adult urban coalitions. They defend their turf against incursions by nonmembers; they build the reputation of the gang by it activities (cellar club, parties, and possession of such prestige items as drugs and weapons); and they purify by trying to drive out incompatible persons.

The neighborhood viewed in terms of the strategies pursued by adults in coalition formation presents a similar picture. These strategies may be roughly defined as defensive, offensive, and purifying. Homogeneous neighborhoods generally follow defensive strategies. This is the common stance of coalitions reasonably satisfied with what they have. The good state of affairs is defined in terms of presently shared characteristics. Therefore, the subject of the coalition is to oppose incursions from the external urban environment which threatens to transform "our neighborhood." The opposition is comprised of those forces which are viewed as changing the neighborhood. Thus, efforts are made to prevent a "different element" from moving in or to prevent the downgrading of zoning. Offensive strategies, on the other hand, involve improvements and enhancements of the particular terrain, so that it becomes attractive to the right kind of people. This is a more difficult coalition to maintain, because it requires expenditures, establishment of clearer goals, and action. This is not to say that offensive strategies are self-conscious displays, created for the benefit of the external world; they may be viewed simply as the expression of the communities' values. Purification involves attempts to root out the incompatible. In residential neighborhoods, this is a difficult task. Slum clearance and urban renewal are examples of radical purification. Purification generally involves the highest cost in conflict, and therefore coalitions organized around this strategy are the hardest to form and maintain.

If neighborhoods form coalitions (many don't), they generally pursue defensive strategies of screening residential applicants.

Racial and class screening tend to occur most frequently, although other, subtle types based on life-style criteria occur also. Because such coalitions call for overt actions, which make them vulnerable to legal redress, screening operations are generally performed by community-based structures rather than by local governments per se. Focus tends to be on control of property purchases, particularly home purchases. The realtors and builders are, of necessity, members of these coalitions because they operate at the point of property purchase or rental. Realtors and builders are dependent upon good will from the community for customers and references. They need favorable attitudes from bankers in order to receive financing of sales and cooperation from city officials in order to gain adjustments in zoning and freedom from harassing regulatory action. Here lies the basis of a tacit coalition in which monetary incentives and public attitudes about proper neighbors are the exchanged values which bind the coalition together. However, any building firm under economic duress can be expected to pull out or try to upset the coalition. A builder does not build houses in keeping with the style of the neighborhood in order to preserve the neighborhood's identity. Ultimately, he builds houses which will sell as rapidly as possible. He merely picks a location where sales are highly promising and the costs are right. However, long-term association with an area involves the necessity of coming to a working agreement with the indigenous community forces which can affect profit levels. Thus, the time horizons of participants influence coalition membership.

An industrial park offers another example of a turf-based coalition. The common bond among members of such a coalition is access to shared services and the maintenance of an environment protected from the contaminating influence of the general urban context. Such coalitions have a membership, a shared set of norms, and a structure for bargaining with other coalitions. Shopping centers, area merchants' associations, chambers of commerce, and industrial development corporations are other kinds of turf coalitions.

Many other domain or turf coalitions could be described, but one is of particular interest to political scientists, that is, the local government. Nearly all local governments have the property of territoriality, but territoriality is not in itself a sufficient condition for a coalition. Some local governments are described by our concept of a coalition, but others are not. Governments provide sets of procedural rules, which control the process of conflict resolution. When they do this, they may be viewed as simply defining the procedural context within which opposing coalitions compete. However, in many situations, a local government does not function simply as a sort of arbiter, but actually joins the urban fray as a coalition.

In a metropolitan setting, the individual local municipalities do not exist in isolation. Governments must continually deal with their external relations to the metropolitan milieu. The suburban municipality must protect its turf. Thus, municipal government may be considered both as a set of procedures for dealing with internal conflict and as a coalition in dealing with the external world. It is probable that the range of stances, coalition in nature, increases with the homogeneity of outlook among the constituents. This very homogeneity may itself be partly derived from a coalition policy in which the municipality defends itself against unwelcome entrants, purifies its membership, and attracts the compatible newcomers through a variety of symbolic stances.

All urban coalitions do not coalesce around maintaining the properties of a particular isolatable space. Sociospatial units have a variety of access requirements, only some of which can be satisfied by controlling the immediate spatial environment. Maintaining access to more remote places is also necessary. Consequently, many urban coalitions focus on the communication network. The time and cost required to move messages, objects, and people over urban space helps to define the utility of urban location. The communication net tends to be locked into rather durable systems, which have powerful influence on the location decisions of sociospatial units. Because communication systems may define the utility of an urban location, changes in the systems often produce great conflict.

Coalitions that form in relationship to communication systems are probably even less durable than those that focus on terrain, partly because the communication systems themselves are relatively fixed and changes are made episodically. Because of the powerful effect of communication systems changes on changing accessibilities, conflicts over proposed changes may become extremely intense. It is only because changes occur at infrequent intervals that such intense conflict is less likely to lead to institutionalization.

In Chapter 2, a parallel was drawn between coalitions and interest groups. A distinction was made then about the relative instability of the urban coalition. Opting out of the latter for an individual is merely a function of moving costs. Changing one's urban coalition membership need not mean forsaking basic preferences or values, whereas, in opting out of an interest group, the individual must be willing to forsake or jeopardize his interests. Thus, urban politics has distinctive qualities which distinguish it from other political arenas, not the least of which is the instability of basic political groups.

All politics at the local governmental level are not coalitional in nature. Non–location-oriented political discourse takes place over a variety of concerns. Issues of tax incidence and service distributions are continual sources of political interchange. Much political action at the state or federal level, as it influences resource redistribution, has implications for sociospatial units and their capacity to achieve success, but such politics does not pertain to the access claims or demands of urban coalition as such. It is possible to aggregate urban access interests explicitly, but we rarely do. A national land development policy, new towns, coordinated transportation development all are examples. The lack of aggregation of urban interests nationally has been another characteristic feature of our nation's urban politics.

National Ideologies and Political Strategy Choices

We have now redefined the three political ways in which sociospatial units may pursue their access goals: (1) by making an adaptive move; (2) by forming a coalition or, occasionally, a community; (3) by engaging in aggregative political activity. These three alternatives may not have the same distributional effects in allocating social access to sociospatial units. One of the significant ways in which variance in a nation's urban policies may be explained is through the differential reliance on these

three political forms. In the United States, the characteristic
urban political act is the move, with coalitions formed occasionally, and aggregation taking place rarely. The result is that
urbanism is seldom treated as a general problem of access, but
instead is particularized into specifics. In a legal sense, state and
federal governments have recently become involved in urban
matters. Whether the resulting programs are indeed new de-
partures in urban politics is yet to be demonstrated.

In some nations, town building, industrial locations, and
regional development are all matters of national policy. In these
situations, some aggregated consideration of urban interests is
present by definition. However, the United States has historically
assigned to local governments jurisdiction over the decisions
which explicitly deal with urban development. Furthermore,
there is a strong ideological justification for maintaining this
decentralization and the preservation of the autonomy of local
governments. The appropriateness of this ideology, derived from
a logic developed over a century and a half ago, is questionable
today.

The ideology of local government was incubated from natural
rights philosophy but assumed a number of practical twists in its
development. The Jeffersonian view, later systematized by
Tocqueville, enshrined local government as a bulwark of freedom.
To Jefferson, legitimate government was based on consent, and
he therefore distrusted representative government. Representatives could easily be subverted when they were away from their
community, and government by consent could be placed in
jeopardy. This led him to elaborate a plan for a four-tiered
government, in which the small ward was the basic unit. The
ward maximized face-to-face confrontations among the vitally
interested parties. Tocqueville's emphasis was slightly different,
and his rhetoric has furnished the underpinnings for most glosses
on behalf of local self-government. Tocqueville, fearing the
tyranny of the majority in the American mass culture, felt that
decentralization was a brake against the mobilization of oppres-
sive majorities. He also admired the robust, pragmatic experi-
mentation exhibited by American local communities, which
contrasted favorably with the stolidness of the continental
peasants, long inured to having problems dealt with by central-

government bureaucrats.[3] Today, this rhetoric becomes "bulwarks against central bureaucracy" and "laboratories of experimentations."

Local self-government for the village on the frontier or for the agricultural service center is one matter, but local self-government for the small suburb in a modern metropolitan context is something completely different, as shall be demonstrated below. However, the strong association of local self-government with a variety of positive political values in the United States has given an ideological foundation for decentralizing control over locational developments. Aggregation of urban concerns is thereby made difficult in this country. When one adds to this fact the entrepreneurial traditions of capitalism, the ideological basis is complete for justifying a heavy reliance on mobility as the primary political form and the transformation of local governments into particularistic coalitions rather than into polities. For as the ideology states, "Local people know the local needs best."

Recapitulation and Illustration

The basic nature of the urban process is the achievement of goals through access gained by persons deploying themselves in space in relationship to other persons. Social access is, in part, made possible by such locations. However, the salience of access is generally related to the context of various roles. The typical day of an urbanite involves physical movement or the changing meaning of place in time, even though a person remains stationary. The desirability or satisfactory nature of one's location at any given time can best be defined in terms of the role occupied by an individual at that time.

Physical location, as an instrumentality of access, is particularly essential for face-to-face interactions. Despite the revolution in communications, face-to-face interactions abound. Certainly the intimate relations of a family have not been reduced to electronically transmitted messages. Shopping, business, sociality, playing, and idling all must involve spatial proximity to others in order for rewarding exchanges to occur. However, physical

[3] Alexis de Tocqueville, *Democracy in America* (New York: Vintage Books, 1960), I, pp. 94–95, 169–170, 273–274, and many other passages.

proximity is neither a necessary nor sufficient condition for access. The street peddler on Wall Street is not linked into the financial center of the nation, except in the most peripheral fashion. It is in terms of role that the salience of the location can be evaluated. The stockbroker role *requires* the Wall Street location, where he *may* buy a vendor's hot dog. The hot dog vendor *requires* customers; he cares little whether or not they are stockbrokers. While our hot dog man and broker find themselves in the same location, that location is more salient for one than for the other.

Because access at a point in time is meaningful to an individual only in terms of a particular role, the unit of urban analysis becomes the system embracing such a role. There is no word in the English language which describes the unit or system which we have called sociospatial. Someone has suggested to the author that the unit should be given a name for the sake of convenience in discourse, and we might honor an illustrious urbanist by calling such a unit a *mumford*. It is, at least, more euphonious than *sociospatial*.

It is recognized that systems which are identified as mumfords may achieve goals through a variety of other strategic acts. When a stock brokerage firm rents an office on Wall Street in order to be more accessible to an information network that will enable it to make money, it is a mumford. When it engages in the process of evaluating the prospective future worth of a stock, it is not. Both acts may be calculated to earn money. The profitability of a firm will increase its resources, and this fact may have relevance for urban analysis, should the firm use its profits to control its access pattern. This distinction is an arbitrary one, but without segmenting social processes, we cannot sufficiently simplify them for study.

Chapter 4

THE
HOUSEHOLD
AND
SOCIAL
ACCESS

Urban Spatial Patterns

In any city, people are located not randomly in time and space, but according to patterns. Some of these patterns are consciously perceived by the inhabitants and are given names such as "downtown," "across the tracks," or "the blue-stocking district." An area place name becomes not only the identifying label of a certain space, but also its social access connotation. At times, these place names take on a national, as well as a local, symbolic meaning; for example, the Bowery, Greenwich Village, Haight-Ashbury, and Sunset Strip. All these identifications recognize the fact that differing spatial distributions exist for various roles and that occupants of particular roles can be further classified into subgroups, which also have particular spatial distributions.

These population distributions are the common dependent variables of urban ecology and geography as efforts are made to explain racial, ethnic, occupational, class, and other types of spatial clustering and changes in clustering over time. By conceiving location as a resource, we can make these concerns more politically relevant, for it then furnishes us with a new accounting unit for measuring the distribution of a utility. Since spatial pattern reflects the use of location for social access, one then needs to ask whether a particular pattern is the result of individual preferences or the product of a system of socially structured power. While the distinction between these two notions is hard to draw, it lies at the heart of most normative judgments about political systems. It is parallel to the distinction between compulsion and choice or elitism and leadership.

It is obvious that there is an unequal distribution of benefits from urban existence or, at least, that there are dissatisfactions with the distribution. Slums and ghettos, as viewed both by their occupants and by outsiders, are seen as socially debilitating and stunting. Congestion, pollution, unsafe streets, delinquency, and distribution of social services (schools, hospitals, care for aged) all manifest themselves in a spatially uneven manner. There are havens and niches in the urban terrain which are relatively problem free, and there are places which must be clearly labeled least desirable.

To this commonplace observation about urban areas, let us add another. Urban growth today is characterized by "sprawl," as existing urban areas are spreading out. For example, much of the state of New Jersey is covered by urbanized areas radiating out from New York and Philadelphia, as well as from a variety of smaller old centers. The New Jersey complex is but part of an urban belt which promises to form a continuous band from southern Maine to Norfolk, Virginia. Similar urban spreads can be found in the Great Lakes region, along the West and Gulf Coasts, and, on a lesser scale, in many other parts of the country. These urban complexes are governed by many political units, which include hundreds of contiguous municipalities, as well as other authorities, special districts, and school districts. Quasi-public and social agency institutions exhibit similar territorial patterns. This is the urban condition generally described as metropolitanism.

It is the contention of this book that there is a reciprocal relationship between these two sets of observations. That is, there is a relationship between the distribution of social benefits derived from urbanism and the decentralization of urban political control. Decentralization of political control favors those who can most easily achieve social access through mobility and penalizes the least mobile. Decentralization also encourages the formation and formalization of terrain-based political coalitions. Finally, given a reliance on mobility and terrain coalitions as the primary forms of urban politics, proposals for centralized political structures usually appear as threatening and antithetical to prevailing interests. Paradoxically, when centralization is employed it is used to preserve the system of decentralized control and not to create an alternative system by which social access is distributed. Any political structure has imbedded in it a value bias, or to use a term more relevant to this context, a distributional tendency. One of the primary objects of urban political analysis is to show the relationships between structures which shape access and value allocations.

Social Areas

For most tabulations or analyses which locate men spatially, data is collected according to family or household roles. The Census of Population records population characteristics according to where people live, not where they work or otherwise spend their time. Furthermore, much additional data is compiled on family units, as, for example, information on heads of households and income and consumption patterns. For our purposes, this means that most census data can be used as indicators of locational patterns of household sociospatial units. In this way, much ecological research and many studies of mobility patterns can help us gain some knowledge of the political strategy of locational choice. The following briefly reviews findings in this area in order to demonstrate how they can be integrated into our framework.

Shevky and Bell found that according to three indices, which they called familism, ethnicity, and social rank, population distributions reflect increased differentiation by social areas, moving from rural areas to the urban center.[1] The ends of the urban-rural continuum were intuitively established as related to population density. Some social process is evidently operating, so that persons identified according to these three indices tend to cluster spatially in cities to a greater degree than is the case in rural areas.

[1] Eshref Shevky and Wendel Bell, *Social Area Analysis* (1955). See also Leslie Kish, "Differentiation in Metropolitan Areas," *American Sociological Review*, 19 (August 1954), pp. 388–398, for a finding of a similar nature.

Social area analysis has been criticized, particularly when it is used as a vehicle for the analysis of individual behavior. What is often referred to as Robinson's dilemma states that one cannot safely draw inferences about individual behavior on the basis of aggregate data on a given population. For our purposes, this is not a problem, since the areal distributions themselves are of interest. However, it is still necessary to determine what areal units are most meaningful. Shevky and Bell, as well as many other students of demography, use the convenient census tract as the basic social area. If all urban politics were simply a matter of adaptive moves, this might serve as well as any small unit. However, if we want to learn about area-based coalitions, it is desirable to analyze population distributions based upon spatially defined political units. While we have not confined our urban coalition concept to local governments, they are certainly the most visible and the ones about which we have the most aggregate data. Consequently, municipalities are our best units for social area analysis.

Early studies of metropolitan areas, which examined the municipality, focused on the differences between the population distributions of core cities and the ring. These studies simply lumped together all suburban municipalities.[2] This choice of areas was primarily guided by the post-World War II political interest in metropolitan governments. Political frictions between core cities and suburbs are not without continued interest, but this dichotomy glosses over more cleavages than it illuminates. The suburbs are neither all the same nor all differentiated from the core city.

More recently, social scientists have begun to treat each municipality as a separate social area. A major initial interest came from public finance, which pointed out the obvious fiscal implications of great variations in the tax base among metropolitan municipalities. Other studies related the differences in mu-

[2] Leo F. Schnore, "The Socio-Economic Status of Cities and Suburbs," *American Sociological Review*, 28 (February 1963), pp. 76–86; Harry Sharp and Leo F. Schnore, "The Changing Color Composition of Metropolitan Areas," *Land Economics*, 38 (May 1962), pp. 168–185; Leo F. Schnore and Harry Sharp, "Racial Changes in Metropolitan Areas, 1950–1960," *Social Forces*, 41 (March 1963), pp. 247–253.

nicipal policy outcomes to variations in their characteristics.[3] These studies take note of the areal specialization displayed by the municipal units of a metropolitan area. Because of the political capacities of municipalities, their specialization is highly significant for control of access.

Despite this growing interest in areal specialization, or, in some cases, segregation patterns, in fact we know very little about changes in metropolitan distributional patterns. As metropolitan areas grow larger, more and more areas are added to the urbanized complex. Is the result more or less areal specialization? Are there characteristic sizes of homogeneous spaces? Is areal specialization changing differentially according to various population characteristics? For example, is there greater social class segregation and age segregation but less income segregation? Some work has been done on race, leading us to believe there is little decline in spatial segregation according to that attribute.[4] When we move from demographic attributes to behavioral patterns, such as style preference, little is known about distributions, let alone about changes in distributions over time.

Even speculatively, it is hard to deduce the direction of change in areal specialization from conventional notions of urban history. The nineteenth-century city was probably more heterogeneous than the twentieth-century city. Diverse people literally had to live on top of one another because of the centripetal forces of the coke-energy-run city. Relatively greater costs of overcoming space friction forced propinquant cohabitation of small spaces by diverse groups. Commercial purveyor and consumer had to be physically proximate. Servants lived near masters. Home and job could not be far apart. Because twentieth-century technology permits persons to expand their daily orbits geographically, one could expect mixed neighborhoods to de-

[3] Seymour Sacks and William Hellmuth, *Financing Government in Metropolitan Areas* (1962); Robert Wood, *1400 Governments* (1961); Oliver Williams, Harold Herman, Charles Liebman, and Thomas Dye, *Suburban Differences and Metropolitan Policies* (1965).

[4] Karl E. Tauber and Alma F. Tauber, *Negroes in Cities: Residential Segregation and Neighborhood Change* (1965); Richard Langendorf, "Residential Desegregation Potential," *Journal of the American Institute of Planners,* 35 (March 1969), pp. 90–95.

cline. The opposite conclusion is also logical. If people are freed from dependence on location, this could lead to more random distributions and areal heterogeneity. Every scrap of descriptive material we have points in the former direction, however.

Spatial Differentiation and Choice Behavior

The social area studies not only are descriptive, but also attempt to be explanatory. Examples such as the Shevky–Bell findings raise questions about the causes of the distributional patterns which they describe. Several attempts have been made to explain the underlying locational choices of households. According to the economic model, the locational choices of sociospatial units are to be understood in terms of rent.[5] While the model may work fairly well for firms, the utility curves of nonprofit units remain problems.[6] If the assumptions of this book are correct, rent purchases not only a building, but also a complex set of social accessibilities. However, models do not exhaust even the economically oriented ways in which locational choices may be explained.

About a decade ago, Charles M. Tiebout published an article called "A Pure Theory of Local Expenditures,"[7] in which he characterized municipalities as service merchants in the pursuit of customers. Each citizen was viewed as having a set of ordered preferences for services, on which he acts within the constraints of his income; while municipalities "compete" for customers by purveying differing market-basket combinations of goods with differing prices (presumably reflecting the quality of the units in the basket). To Tiebout, this model was usable as a basis of analysis. It goes without saying that Tiebout had a metropolitan area, not simply a local government, in mind. Only in the governmentally fragmented metropolitan areas is it possible to shop for

[5] William Alonso, "A Theory of the Urban Land Market," *Regional Science Association, Papers and Proceedings*, vol. 6, 1960, pp. 149–158.

[6] See Michael A. Stegman, "Accessibility Models and Residential Location," *Journal of the American Institute of Planners*, 35 (January 1969), pp. 22–29.

[7] Charles M. Tiebout, "A Pure Theory of Local Expenditures," *Journal of Political Economy*, LXIV (October 1956), pp. 416–424.

a municipality, in a service-consumer sense. In isolated small towns, municipal services are a monopoly. Only in a metropolitan area, can one maintain one's job and still choose among a variety of municipalities in selecting a domicile.

In a subsequent article with Ostrom and Warren, Tiebout's idea was extended explicitly to metropolitan areas.[8] Not only was municipal policy diversity treated as a response to consumer-citizen demands, but also the diversity of governmental arrangements themselves. Because of economies of scale and service area problems, some demands cannot be met by municipalities. Thus, ad hoc larger governmental structures emerge to take care of special cases. For example, complete specialization in the service bundles is not feasible because of the reciprocal effect of one municipality's policies on another's (mosquito and ragweed control) or the difficulties of decentralizing (water and highway systems). Thus, not only specialization but cooperation (voluntary and involuntary) were looked upon as a kind of adaptation by a complex set of adjacent governments to a set of consumer demands.

Many studies of why people move fail to support the economic market hypothesis; at least, some survey findings do not. Rossi's study[9] as well as Gans' case study of Levittown[10] both stress that community related factors were less influential in housing choices than were the physical attributes of the dwelling itself. However, there are a number of offsetting pieces of evidence which lead one to doubt that people choose houses in a fashion similar to the way they select cars or refrigerators. Of the total moves, a certain number represent changes in family structure through marriage, divorce, additional children, or death. Persons with similar needs may gravitate toward similar places without being conscious of the commonalty of their orientation. It is clear some decisions to move grow out of dissatisfaction with the old neighborhood. Crime in the streets, changing neighborhoods, and increased income, which alters consumption prac-

---

[8] Vincent Ostrom, Charles M. Tiebout and Robert Warren, "The Organization of Government in Metropolitan Areas: A Theoretical Inquiry," *American Political Science Review*, 55 (December 1961), pp. 831–842.

[9] Peter Rossi, *Why People Move* (1955).

[10] Herbert Gans, *The Levittowners* (1967).

tices, are all the basis of a negative decision on continued residence.[11]

While the overt-response survey data seemingly cast doubt on the community-service, market-basket selection of municipalities, the combination of house cost, style, and location may, in fact, create guided paths that sort out the population and channel homogeneous populations to common destinations. Persons may shop for a house and ignore its environment, but the choices made must lie within the limits of given resources. In addition, notions of style are gained from reference groups, and information is exchanged through friendship patterns. For all these reasons, we should be skeptical of the findings of "why-people-move" studies which report that people shop for houses, not communities.[12]

A number of studies give further, though fragmentary, evidence to support this doubt. One suggests that the whole structure of individual utility functions in housing choices may be class based. Duncan and Duncan found that white-collar workers allocate larger percentages of their household budgets to housing than do blue-collar workers.[13] Whether for this or other reasons, they also found that various occupations tended to cluster spatially in their selection of residential places. Laumann has investigated associations generally in urban areas. He established the strong tendency for friendships to be drawn from similar occupational groups; this was particularly true for persons in the high- and low-status extremes.[14] He found the same to be true about household propinquity, even though 72 percent of the urban respondents stated that they did not know their neighbors

[11] Richard S. Lamanna, "Values Consensus Among Urban Residents," *Journal of the American Institute of Planners,* 30 (November 1964), p. 321, found that what people want most in an "ideal" community are those things which they do not presently enjoy but which they desire.

[12] For some studies which focus on neighborhood choices per se, see John B. Lansing, *Residential Location and Urban Mobility* (1966); Robert L. Wilson, "Liveability of the City: Attitudes and Urban Development," in F. Stuart Chapin and Shirley F. Weiss (eds.), *Urban Growth Dynamics* (1962).

[13] Otis Dudley Duncan and Beverly Duncan, "Residential Distribution and Occupational Stratification," *American Journal of Sociology,* 60 (March 1965), p. 493.

[14] Edward O. Laumann, *Prestige and Association in an Urban Community* (1966), pp. 66–67.

or knew them only casually.[15] Despite the low level of knowledge about neighbors, the probability was high that neighbors in the high and low occupational status categories would be of a similar occupational status. Feldman and Tilly found that education was even more important than occupation in explaining residential choices in a Hartford study.[16] This finding is supported by the work of Coke and Liebman, who investigated two Philadelphia suburbs which were physically proximate and had similarly priced new homes.[17] Home purchasers in the two areas appeared to divide along social rank lines, even though income was presumably constant for the two groups.

Thus, despite the findings of Rossi and Gans that people buy houses, not communities, objective evidence of actual distributions indicates that some life style considerations contribute to a sorting-out process. It may well be that people are not attracted to a house specifically for the casual neighboring it will provide. For example, it is highly likely that social acquaintances of high status persons will be widely dispersed geographically. A judicious choice of a house may assure that accepted low levels of neighboring will be respected by those around because they will have similar life styles. On the other hand, lower status people are more likely to feel at home where neighboring takes the form of mutual help through borrowing, baby sitting, house watching, and shopping. Just because higher status persons are less dependent on neighbors for help and sociality, it does not mean they do not use location for access. Areal homogeneity also protects one from unwanted neighboring.

There is some evidence that when relatively heterogeneous populations *do* move into a spatial community, particularly into a new one, conflict over policies emerges, and a sorting-out process sets in when these conflicts become manifest. In Gans's study of Levittown, the population originally assembled was essentially the rational house bargain hunters. The price range qualified persons in both skilled blue-collar as well as white-collar jobs for

[15] *Ibid.*, p. 72.
[16] Arnold S. Feldman and Charles Tilly, "The Interaction of Social and Physical Space," *American Sociological Review,* 25 (December 1960), pp. 877–84.
[17] James Coke and Charles Liebman, "Political Values and Population Density Controls," *Land Economics,* 37 (November 1961), pp. 347–361.

home purchases. Conflicts over service priorities developed as soon as community organizations were established.[18] Catholic versus Protestant differences, as well as class conflicts, developed over schools. Dobriner records a similar division in Levittown, New York, where a middle-class population was being supplanted by a blue-collar one.[19] There, the misunderstanding, which seemed to be rooted in differing life styles, led eventually to gross mutual mistrust, and accusations were made of subversion and communism. If social conflict contributes to dissatisfaction with neighborhood, mobility may gradually convert heterogeneous neighborhoods into homogeneous ones.

In the studies by Gans and Dobriner, conflict was manifest in the context of a community structure. It was when value choices were made explicit that the battle was enjoined. This overt conflict stage is probably not necessary for the creation of spatial division among disagreeing groups. Fogelson notes in his history of Los Angeles that zoning laws and deed restrictions prevented the intermixture of divergent income groups in residential areas. He feels that social homogeneity was achieved in spatial areas prior to community formation, and as a result community organization never developed.[20]

Some work has been done on the psychological stresses which may exist in heterogeneous communities. Examples are found in the work of Peter Willmott in his studies of Dagenham, Bethnal Green, and Woodford.[21] In these, it is quite clear that the most frequent expressions of disquiet occur in the mixed neighborhoods. On the other hand, the inhabitants of the massive one-class Dagenham are blissfully secure in their unchallenged, uniformly working-class haven.

From the foregoing, it seems clear that subcultures of our urban populations, which have similar access requirements, tend

[18] Gans, *op. cit.*, pp. 92–100, 116–122; see also S. D. Clark, *The Suburban Society* (1966), pp. 211ff. for a description of a similar process in Toronto suburbs.

[19] William Dobriner, *Class in Suburbia*, (1963), pp. 85–126.

[20] Robert M. Fogelson, *Fragmented Metropolis: Los Angeles, 1850–1930* (1967), p. 194.

[21] Peter Willmott, *The Evolution of a Community* (1963), and *Family and Class in a London Suburb* (1960); and Michael Young and Peter Willmott, *Family and Kinship in East London* (1957).

to cluster spatially. The clusters, however, are not all easy to name or identify. The nineteenth-century city had its social mosaic of ethnic neighborhoods, where linguistic factors, as well as social nurture, required propinquity. Acculturation has largely eroded these groups, with some conspicuous exceptions. Even though ethnicity may be a durable trait, which continues to mark individuals into the fourth and fifth generation, the neighborhood requirement certainly need not contribute to it beyond the second or third.[22] If there is a contemporary social life which involves spatial segregation, it is within a framework of what may be properly called "American."

Gans claims that there are working- and middle-class subcultures in our society and identifiable subsets of each.[23] His portrayal of the peer group socialization process nearly guarantees the impossibility of heterogeneous middle- and working-class neighborhoods in large urban complexes. One of the clear differences between the heterogeneous metropolis and the heterogeneous small town is that in the latter fairly clear interpersonal hierarchies exist, hierarchies maintained through a variety of primary relations. Such circumstances are unlikely to endure in a large mobile metropolis.

Social class may not suffice in identifying the subcultures. We may need a concept—such as Agger's "sense of cultural class," which may be related to, but is not synonymous with, social class—in order to describe the population patterns.[24] Historical modes of expression, capacity to project into roles of others, perceptions of status, and object and person orientation may constitute the ingredients of a common sense of cultural class, which makes people feel at home or not at home in a particular place. While modern technology in communications and transportation has greatly reduced the importance of propinquity, the fact remains that all social arrangements must eventually come down to the ground; they happen within space on this earth. Those who count politically in any local arena are those who recognize

[22] Parenti, op. cit.
[23] Herbert Gans, The Urban Villager (1962).
[24] Robert Agger, Daniel Goldrich, and Bert Swanson, The Rulers and the Ruled (1964).

this fact. Such an urban citizen articulates and exposes his sense of style to others nearby, and from the ensuing interactions local policies are developed. The abdicating local citizen is substantially dependent for the maintenance of his environment on the actions of others.

It would appear that under certain conditions there are incompatible groups that have great difficulty cohabiting in peace, which should lead, in time, to areal differentiation among urban populations. To the extent that diverse populations have diverse preferences for local policies, there should be variations in policies among local governments and other territorially based bodies.[25] Logic suggests that this would produce a feedback effect in reenforcing the segregation process.

Individual Attributes and Spatial Homogeneity

A variety of case and statistical studies of urban areas suggests a set of hypotheses about population characteristics and spatial homogeneity. We can specify the kinds of persons or households likely to seek homogeneous spatial areas and the kinds who will find it less important.

It is commonplace now in the United States for persons to live in different communities in the course of their lives. Most urban Americans do not live in the same neighborhood as adults in which they lived as children. If we think of the neighboring requirements of families in different stages of their life cycle and resource constraints, we can posit differences in each stage with respect to their neighborhood preferences. Figure 2 portrays a likely set of relationships between life cycle and tolerance of, or attraction to, the homogeneity-heterogeneity differences of neighborhoods. The curve is based upon the assumption that young married and childless couples are fairly free-floating urban citizens, who depend very little on propinquity for access and starting salaries tend to equalize resources across occupational classes.

[25] See the author's book with Harold Herman, Charles Liebman, and Thomas Dye, *op. cit.* This book investigated the relationship between aggregate municipal characteristics and municipal outcomes in the Philadelphia metropolitan area.

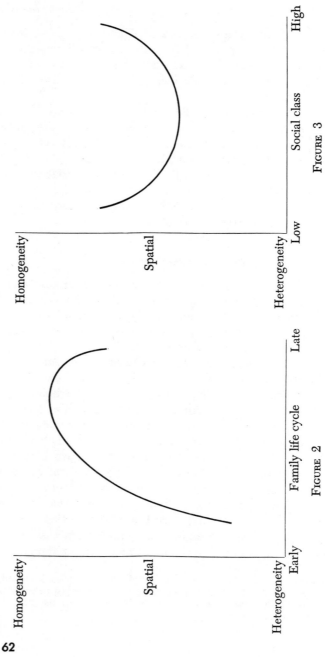

Homogeneity

Spatial

Heterogeneity

Early   Family life cycle   Late

FIGURE 2

Homogeneity

Spatial

Heterogeneity

Low   Social class   High

FIGURE 3

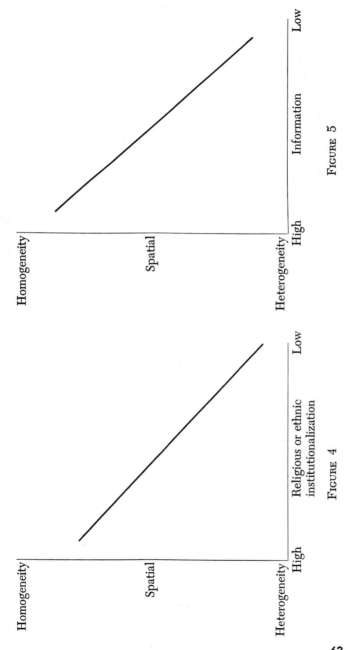

FIGURE 4

FIGURE 5

63

Divergent views on child rearing practices tend to make spatially homogeneous neighborhoods most preferred in the middle years of married life. Later there may be a great deal of toleration of heterogeneity, although probably very little attraction by it. Old people find it hard to move. Their lives are more circumscribed by routine, and social interactions are less numerous with advancing years. It is probable that neighborhood heterogeneity, in a demographic sense, is increased by the relatively lower mobility of aged populations.

Figure 3 suggests the relationship between tolerance of, and/or attraction to, heterogeneity and social class. We have some evidence to support the notion (Laumann) that great congruence of social and spatial distances occurs particularly at each end of the social class scale. Industrial society creates ambiguities over the middling range. One of the interesting comparative urban studies yet to be made is the investigation of variation in urban status segregation in different national cultures.

A third relationship which is suggested in Figure 4 is that between homogeneity and the degree of religious and ethnic institutionalization. Not all religious or ethnic minorities cluster. However, institutions, such as schools and churches, often require propinquity. Although it is possible, with some investment, to rely on such institutions from considerable distance, if intensive involvement is required, propinquity is essential (e.g., Williamsburg in Brooklyn). Because of the absence of religious data from the census, we do not know about religious distribution in suburbs. Jewish and Catholic suburbs are popularly identified. In Canada, segregation between Anglo and French persons is pronounced and made apparent by linguistic identification.

Specific sociospatial units may be caught in cross pressures from identifications that pull in differing directions. Such cross pressures may impede the development of homogeneous social areas. Spatial mobility is affected by a number of non–preference- or non–value-related factors, like resources and politics. The distribution of economic resources places obvious limits on the choice available. An interesting question is the effect of differences in available information resources. We know very little about the social area map in the heads of urban dwellers. How well-informed are the actors in the urban ecological drama? One would think that older and more stable urban areas would afford greater clarity of place identification in the public mind. It seems reasonable to assume that European city dwellers have rather widely shared social area maps of their metropolitan areas. Probably this is truer for older and Eastern cities in the United States than for the newer Western and Southern developing ones in California, Texas, and Florida. Figure 5 suggests this relationship which may help in explaining intercity differences.

Chapter **5**

ENTREPRENEURSHIP
AND
URBANISM

The decisions of economic entrepreneurs are a major force in the shaping of American cities. There are two quite different sets of entrepreneurial decisions involved. First, entrepreneurship satisfies certain access requirements through locational strategies. That is, each firm's leadership must decide where to locate various of the firm's components in order to reduce the cost of overcoming space friction. Because such decisions determine place of work, they constitute a major force in shaping cities. Secondly, some firms are in the business of merchandising urban access itself; they develop urban environments and sell them to others. It is with this second type of entrepreneurship that we shall be primarily concerned in this chapter.

The Merchandising of Access

The land and development merchants have always been major actors in American urban development. Because of the speculative nature of part of their profits, urban land investors have been frequent objects of criticism the world over. Because speculative gain is created by civilization, rather than by the actual combining of the owner's labor with the land, many have advocated, and some nations have tried, the socialization of these unearned increments. Thus, today, in most European nations, the private urban developer has his discretion narrowly circumscribed, while in most of the nations of the Western Hemisphere, cities are still built largely through private entrepreneurship.

In order to understand the role of entrepreneurship in the development of United States cities, it is essential to understand the interaction between the regulatory structure and the city-building industry. The city-building industry remains the largest industry still essentially regulated at the lowest governmental level. The industry includes the builders, developers, engineers, real estate owners, and realtors, along with their financiers and lawyers. The instruments of regulation include zoning, subdivision controls, official maps, comprehensive plans, building and fire codes, building permits, and a miscellany of other minor regulations. In addition, new urban developments have to be attached to systems which service structures. These land serving systems include water, sewers, streets, power, and telephones, some of which are privately managed. The urban utility systems and their regulation are generally the responsibility of the lowest level of government, though no generalization can be made which is completely accurate in all fifty states.

The many branches of the city-building industry interact with the many regulatory bodies in a great variety of settings. We can get a better overview of this interaction by classifying the circumstances under which regulation most commonly takes place. A major difference usually exists between new development on the fringes and redevelopment of previously built-up areas.

Fringe area development

Most additions to our urban space take place on the edges of existing metropolitan areas. What is the context here in which regulator and regulated meet? Let us consider the legal status of the fringe area, the "constitutional" constituency of the new area and the aspirations of the constitutional constituents.

The legal status of fringe areas varies considerably across the country. The basic difference, however, is between the Northeastern and Midwestern States on the one hand, which inherited the town and township tradition of local government, and the

Southern and Western States on the other, which have historically relied upon the municipality and county as the basic local
units. These different traditions were established over a century
ago along the eastern seaboard, as the states tried to solve the
problem of devising governments for both rural and urban areas.
The towns and townships, like counties, were originally designed
as rural units of government, but they are much smaller than
counties. Though originally rural units, most of them have now
acquired urban types of regulatory powers, such as zoning and
other land development controls. As a metropolitan area expands
into the countryside, these preexisting small towns or townships,
which lie in the path of urban expansion, become the effective
political arena in which regulation of the urban entrepreneurial
industries takes place.

Along the eastern seaboard, and through most of the Great
Lakes states, there are literally hundreds of these rural townships
on the urban frontier, which deal each day with the advance men
of the urban future; that is, the speculator, the developer, and
their agents. These sparsely settled rural townships first feel the
impact of the coming city through a kind of scattered population fallout. Individuals willing to endure a long commute in
exchange for a rustic home environment begin buying up lots
along back roads and highways. School populations grow and
traffic increases. Suddenly, one day the town government is faced
with a subdivider, and then the urban "constitutional" phase for
that little sector, the township on the urban frontier, begins. The
way in which the township responds to these early decisions may
well foretell what is to come. At some critical point, the social
meaning of the area will be substantially established for the first
generation of urban inhabitation, and no wishful statements in
the form of a revamped zoning ordinance will change the future
pattern of development.

These attempts to define the future by zoning take several
forms. The most typical strategy is to build a dam against the
future by zoning land either as all industrial or as extremely low-
density residential of from two- to five-acre minimum lot size.
Each township which does this says, in effect, if the city must
come, it should come either in the form of rich people with
large, expensive homes on beautifully landscaped grounds or in

the form of high performance industrial plants, which have similarly well-manicured grounds, cause no traffic congestion, and emit no noise, smoke, odor, glare, or industrial waste.

Because most people and most firms do not conform to these high standards, the urban entrepreneurs must break the regulatory bonds. If new homes, apartments, stores, and factories are to be built, they must be matched to the characteristics and the access requirements of the buyers. Thus, the merchants of urbanization must take on the township regulators, and they do so on a parcel-by-parcel basis. The usual strategy involves some form of cooptation of indigenous businessmen, such as the lawyers, realtors, or bankers. The objective for the urban entrepreneur is a sale. He must convince some buyer that a particular place will provide the opportunity for the right combination of social accessibilities. Each sale introduces new constituents into the regulator polity, sometimes facilitating, or sometimes inhibiting, the permeability of the township for entrance by the next entrepreneur.

Each township usually goes through a series of political upheavals, the first of which centers around the old-timers and the newcomers. Dobriner has described the process, which John Updike treated fictionally.[1] The newcomers disrupt and destroy a previously existing community, but they also bring wealth in the form of customers for merchants and increased prices for land. The old-timers usually hang on to political control longer than their numbers would explain because they are familiar with the paraphernalia of local government, while the newcomers are more concerned, at the outset, with the problems of nesting down. It is inevitable that the first formative decisions are made by the old-timers. Thus, to the extent that the kind of regulation exercised guides growth at all, the decisions are made by a political group, nonurban in background, which will not likely inhabit the urban environment to which it gives initial definition.

All metropolitan areas are not ringed by previously existing town and township governments. In the South and West, the urban fringe is usually a no man's land of unincorporated terri-

---

[1] William M. Dobriner, *Class in Suburbia* (1963). See Chapter 5 in particular.

tory. The development pattern in the broadest terms may not be very much different from that under the townships, but the regulatory constituency is formally quite different.

Land use regulations in unincorporated fringe areas are under the jurisdiction of the county, but a metropolitan county government is a most peculiar political entity. In such a county, most of the urbanized areas will usually be incorporated into municipalities. These municipalities, of course, regulate the urban entrepreneurs within their boundaries. Each incorporated municipality will have its zoning and planning commission and the whole regulatory paraphernalia. The bulk of the county population is usually within one of these municipalities, often including a core city and a number of incorporated suburbs. The county government regulates development on the fringe, where there are no or few people.

But who are the constituents of the county regulators? County governments are amorphous and inconspicuous things. The more visible local units of government are the municipalities. In a metropolitan county, there may be ten to a hundred separate governments in the business of regulating urban development, and the county will be but one of them. Coordination or mutual understandings among the various units is more the exception than the rule. The county planning commission or zoning board will have a very peculiar constituency, because the fringe area developments are unlikely to engage the intense interests of the citizens in any but the most adjacent built-up areas. Like many regulatory bodies which are out of the public scrutiny, they, in fact, become closely identified with the interests of the urban entrepreneurs themselves.

To further complicate matters, a variety of things can happen to redefine the regulatory jurisdictions in the fringe no man's land. Unincorporated areas can be annexed by adjacent municipalities, or new municipalities can be carved out of unincorporated territory if they meet certain set state requirements as to size and density. Developers, land owners, and affected residents can then engage in an elaborate coalitional struggle to define who regulates what terrain. Boundary manipulation on the metropolitan fringe is a great American urban pastime, played with particular adroitness and sophistication in the growing metropolitan areas of Florida, California, Michigan, and Texas.[2]

Reuse and Recycling

The pattern of social access is never static in any urban area. While change is continuous, there are critical turning points in which the basic social meaning of places is altered. At such times, it is not simply a matter of one set of inhabitants replacing another; the values associated with places change. Eventually there comes a time when a place loses social meaning and value. Then, short of some private or public intervention, vacancy, deterioration, and decay follow.

Our laws are written so that we monitor the urban process when the use of land is changed from one legal category to another or when some physical alteration is made in buildings or terrain. The major monitoring instrument is the zoning ordinance.[3] Most of our metropolitan core cities were built without the benefit of such an ordinance, but they have had such ordinances passed after the fact. Zoning is supposedly a means of guiding growth, but in the old core cities, it can only be a guide to the recycling of land use. It is really a very crude instrument for this purpose; what it really does is give cities the legal right to monitor changes. Zoning usually begins by writing the existing land use into an ordinance, so that any proposal for change requires a legal change in the ordinance and therefore must be processed by some legal-political body. Some cities pass zoning ordinances which describe the way the ordinance writers wish that the city had been built in the first place. This is a rather pretentious representation of planning, but it leads to practically the same place as patterning the ordinance after existing usages.

---

[2] See Winston W. Crouch and Beatrice Dinerman, *Southern California Metropolis* (1963); and Robert D. Warren, *Government in Metropolitan Regions* (1966), for accounts of competitive incorporations. Municipalities can also be carved out of township territories in most Eastern states, as similar boundary manipulations occur there as well.

[3] Sidney Willhelm, *Urban Zoning and Land Use Theory* (1962), analyzes the zoning decisional process in Austin, Texas. His data support much that is said about zoning decisions in the passages which follow.

In either case, most proposals for change will fail to conform to the zoning ordinance in some respect, so each change requires a legal permission.

Most recycling of land can be described most realistically as a filtering down process. Big houses are broken up into apartments, and old factories are subdivided for warehouses or for marginal industries requiring cheap, low-grade space. The major function of the regulatory process is to determine whether the neighbors object to this filtering down. Depending on the style of politics, some heed may be paid to the objectors, or a political levy may be exacted from the requester. The filtering process goes on constantly in almost all developed areas a generation old, and each jurisdiction has a set of local entrepreneurs whose major service is in knowing how to process requests for change.

Recycling is one of the least understood of our urban processes. We have long been aware of slums, and much effort has been expended to eliminate them. The urban renewal clearance program, one such effort, indicates the need to pay attention to the social meaning of place in all urban planning.

The clearance idea was based on the admitted failure of private entrepreneurship as the agency for recycling urban land. It was felt that the capitalization of profits into the values of slum properties prevented their prices from dropping to a point where private venture capital could move in, buy, and build something new. This was the premise of the original heart-of-the-slums strategy used in the early fifties. City after city cleared its worst residential slum areas, wrote down the cost of the land, and then offered it to private developers. There were no takers. The problem was that a deteriorated area was, by definition, a place which was least desired as a location to provide social access; it was not simply an area of worn-out houses. This was particularly true for any would-be tenant who could afford to rent in a new structure. The locations were most accessible to new slums, created by the exodus of people from the clearance areas, the low-wage industries, the poor commercial services, an ugly environment, and an objectionable set of local services. The land often lay fallow for years, only to be eventually filled by public works projects, including public housing, all uses which could be completely defined by an ordinance.

In the second wave of redevelopment, the question asked was what places had a high access value, for which willing private developers could be found. Whether or not the land could be defined as sufficiently deteriorating to qualify for the federal blight standards was a secondary question. The places which did provide the demanded access became sites of the projects that "paid off."

Politics and Entrepreneurship

Both private and public redevelopment projects, particularly the large ones, must run the gauntlet of the local urban regulators. We really do not know whether this gauntlet represents simply the levying of a political toll or whether it is a process which expresses social preferences. Stated differently, the regulatory process can be one of three things: (1) The process is effectively neutral, and projects for which the merchants of access have customers will be built. A political toll may be exacted, but this has little effect on what will and what will not be built; (2) the process operates in terms of civic priorities, and authorizations are only granted for projects that conform to a plan or to some politically defined priorities; (3) the process is essentially corrupt, and projects are built which profit the controllers of the regulatory process.

The same questions can be asked about the urban process generally. If the first model is correct, the urban regulatory structure is meaningless because economic resources determine the outcome. The second alternative maintains that regulation can at least bend or distort the market in terms of some specifiable community norms. The third model treats the regulators as entrepreneurs as well and states that they manipulate the system in order to maximize the rate of exaction. In all three models, it is assumed, of course, that some kind of marketing and merchandising process goes on, the only question being what its allocating bias is.

One of the great needs in urban analysis is for formal models which will enable us to answer these kinds of questions. Unfortunately, there are no such models to present here; however, we can gain certain clues from the structure of interaction between merchants of urban access and their regulators. It would seem that we operate fairly closely to the first alternative, with only occasional distortions from politics, both clean and corrupt. The reasons stem from two characteristics of the regulatory structure: First, the structure is highly decentralized and, second, it is handled largely in terms of bargaining.

The decentralized nature of the process simply reflects the political fragmentation of local governments. This fragmentation operates not only across governments, as in the metropolitan case, but also within governments. There are few cities or counties in the United States which have been able to coordinate their urban transforming agencies, such as their planning commissions, zoning boards of adjustment, code enforcement agencies, courts, school districts, public works departments, and highway departments. The most insulated of these agencies are usually the courts and the highway builders, as both are usually tied to state-wide constituencies. The clientele orientation of bureaucracies is as operative here as elsewhere in governments.

The second characteristic of the regulatory process is that it is handled in an adversary or bargaining fashion.[4] When a proposal is made for a zoning variance, a zoning amendment, a new high school, or a renewal project, the contest is between the sponsors and those who feel immediately and adversely affected. The opposing groups appear before the relevant boards armed with petitions and lawyers. In many cases, even the city government will appear simply as a contestant. The spatially proximate property owners and prospective developers are the primary private parties at issue. This definition of the legal public is often stressed by laws which require the posting of notices on the physical properties for which alteration is proposed.

In summary, in decisions about changing the urban environment the relevant public with standing is initially circumscribed through decentralization. This means that the regulators who are the official representatives of the public interest will have very narrow constituencies. The relevant public is further constricted by the way standing is defined in a de facto sense. In the metropolitan context, which has such a great number and range of

---

[4] See Edward Banfield, *Political Influence* (1961), for a series of case studies which illustrate the kind of decisions discussed here.

regulatory arenas, there is actually a marketplace of regulations. The "buyer" can choose the community with the properly permissive set of rules.

The regulators do have a number of public interest maxims, such as "highest and best use" and "in accordance with the comprehensive plan." It is questionable whether these really are durable instruments or criteria for making decisions. Willhelm found that both the citizens and the members of the zoning board of adjustment in Austin, Texas, were guided essentially by their own values and interests and that they expressed these views in terms of perceptions of the social meaning of space.[5]

It would appear that the only circumstance where the third model could operate effectively is where a particular place has a monopoly over access. There may be certain urban places of great strategic value, for which there are few good alternatives. In these cases, political blackmail may work. At one time, the central business district was such a place, and in a few cities, it may still be. Large immobile institutions, such as hospitals and universities, which can only expand into adjacent space, are politically vulnerable. But highly valued access places, for which there are no substitutes, are probably on the decline.

What of the second alternative, the one which embodies the idea of democratically controlled urban planning? Given the structure of the regulatory process, it would appear that political control over the urban market is largely a matter of shunting certain uses from one place to another, rather than of guiding the overall urban form.

The Firm as a Socio-spatial Unit.

Economic entrepreneurship in urban areas is largely concerned with the consumption of access not with the merchandising of it. A firm is a bundle of sociospatial units, each of which is linked into the urban environment. Because the access requirements internal to a firm are likely to be great, firms often house all their components under one roof, thus reducing the cost of overcoming space friction. But this may not be, and most frequently is not, the optimum arrangement, and an entrepreneurial

[5] Willhelm, *op. cit.* See Chapter 14 in particular.

decision is made concerning deployment of components to various locations. Most firms, in fact, separate office areas from production or warehousing. The more complex the firm, the greater the likelihood that its various components will require different sets of accessibilities to the urban environment.

One of the older traditions in location economics explains spatial distributions of firms in terms of cost of overcoming space friction and the price of acquiring a location. Haig formulated this view into a set of hypotheses about forty years ago. His first hypothesis stated that a rational firm will try to reduce its cost for overcoming space friction.[6] Because the desire lines of many economic units might converge on the same location, Haig's second hypothesis was that the firm which could exploit a given location for the greatest profit would occupy it. Stated differently, the firm which could pay the highest rent would occupy a space. For example, office buildings, which can yield enormous rents for a parcel of land, inevitably can buy out other would-be users of central city locations.

Most descriptions of locational tendencies of metropolitan area firms indicate that not only manufacturing but also commerce and services are moving out of core areas. Suburbanization is certainly not simply a residential phenomenon.[7] The reduction of dependence for access on fixed locations has transformed the whole suburbanization process. The electronic transmittal of both standardized and nonstandardized messages has greatly reduced the proportionate need for face-to-face meetings. Dependence on fixed rail and wharf locations characterizes a declining component of manufacturing and industry activities as the principal products have changed from heavy capital goods to smaller items, diversified inventories, information, and services.

While Haig's hypotheses may still be sound today, the underlying variables have changed radically. The first hypothesis refers to the cost of overcoming space friction, but does not specify the objects of access. For example, while at one time industries were

[6] R. M. Haig, *Major Economic Factors in Metropolitan Growth and Arrangement* (1928).

[7] One of the most thorough case study documentations of suburbanization processes is contained in the ten-volume report of the New York Metropolitan Region Study, which was edited by Raymond Vernon. The summary volume is Raymond Vernon, *Metropolis 1985* (1960).

a magnet which drew workers to them, it may now be that industries also pursue the labor force, causing a reciprocal feedback affecting the locational relationship between the two factors. In addition, it may well be that the cost of overcoming space friction represents a declining percentage of total costs or that, at least, the proportion of total costs which can be reduced through an urban locational strategy is declining. Perhaps we are beginning to see the birth of the footloose firm, which is free from metropolitan connections in terms of material inputs or outputs or external economies and must consider only its labor force. A research firm, working on government contracts, may provide an example: It may locate in some resort-like clime, fitting the fancy of those who must come together daily to produce the research product.

Haig's second hypothesis may also be sound, but there is no doubt about the changing spatial distribution of rents. Land rents have been represented topographically in terms of cost per square unit and portrayed as peaks and valleys on a plane. The nineteenth century city had a precipitous peak in the CBD (Central Business District), with lesser peaks around wharves and rail heads. While the CBD peak remains, it is greatly eroded in most cities; and, in the near future, some of those peaks may, indeed, become valleys, because the new shopping center form of organization is vitiating the function of the old downtown areas.

With a wider distribution of the points of favored access, and hence higher rents, there is also a wider distribution of regulatory power. The power of the Victorian city boss was, in part, enhanced by the ecological structure of the city and the dependence of the entire urban social organization on central facilities. With a highway-oriented transportation system, as well as the technological revolution in communications, the monopoly situation is declining.

The new decentralized political form practically removes industry from the regulatory clout. Tax base starved local municipalities can be counted on to compete for industries and commercial operations. To most local officials, industry is a "paying" proposition, because it brings in more in the form of property taxes than it costs in municipal services. There are much lore and many rules of thumb about break-even, profitable, and deficit land uses. All but the lowest grade industry is usually courted. This suggests that industry, of all sociospatial units, finds the least political resistance to its movement.

The urban expressway systems do create high access nodes, which place some political regulators between the entrepreneur and their most desired location. The placing of these nodes is usually formally decided upon by the state highway department. While municipalities may participate in the design process, they cannot always control the decisions. Once the facility is built, those communities which contain major interchanges probably are in a position to make a real choice. Given its new high access location, such a municipality is suddenly in a seller's market. One would expect that merchants of consumer goods (shopping center developers) would be a most politically active group in those suburbs. The first law of merchandising is getting to the customer. It may well be that he who gets his shopping center in first will get the customers and that there are not infinite alternatives.

Summary

In this chapter we have been concerned with the patterns of interaction between urban entrepreneurs and their regulators. In a highly diffused and decentralized regulatory system which has developed, it is hard to see what values prevail. It has been suggested that under such a decentralized arrangement, economic rather than political resources are advantaged. While there is a very intense interaction between entrepreneurs and regulatory groups (some would say that suburban politics is equivalent to zoning plus schools), it is more difficult to say that the marketplace has been abridged in any real sense by the urban regulators. While islands of homogeneity are indeed built, the flood of the urban tide seeks its own course for the most part unimpeded by local regulation.

Chapter 6

CENTRALIZATION
AND
DECENTRALIZATION
OF
METROPOLITAN
POLITICS

We have discussed the behavior and strategies of individual coalitions and the responses of individual governments in the American metropolitan setting. However, we have not given any attention to the overall pattern of governments in metropolitan areas. The general pattern is one of decentralized responsibility to the individual municipal and school district level. Overlaying this decentralization is a complex of intergovernmental cooperative arrangements and more or less inclusive arrangements for specific functional areas. Finally, there are cases of interlevel intervention in selected areas. Is this arrangement simply a historical accumulation? How can it be accounted for? There have been various efforts to account for this, but they have not been altogether satisfactory. In this chapter we will apply the locational-social access approach to illustrate its usefulness in urban analysis. The central thesis of this chapter is that formal governmental decentralization is the outcome of dependence on mobility and coalitions for the distribution of urban utilities.

The Pattern of Government in the Metropolis

Those who are familiar with the pattern of government in American metropolitan areas may wish to skip this immediate section. However, for those who are not, it is essential for understanding the organizing question—which is to follow.

The characteristic of governments in metropolitan areas is

fragmentation. In the official list of 212 Standard Metropolitan Statistical Areas in 1963, there were 18,442 local governments, or an average of 87 local governments per SMSA. The 24 SMSA's with populations over 1,000,000 had, on the average, 301 local governments, but even the smaller SMSA's (populations between 50,000 and 1,000,000) had an average of 24. Metropolitan areas, for this reason, have been described as a crazy quilt of local governments. Over half the governments are school or special districts, and the rest are general purpose local governments, such as municipalities, towns, or townships. Most of the new cities and special districts which come into being annually occur in Standard Metropolitan Areas. Few municipalities go out of existence. Some adjustment among special districts takes place through consolidations and extensions, but the total number of urban-based special districts is increasing. The only exception is school districts, now being reduced in number through state departments of education programs, which encourage consolidation into districts large enough to support comprehensive high schools.

Beginning in the twenties and thirties, various observers of the city scene in the United States recognized this emerging fragmented governmental pattern. Actually, the first suburbs and satellite cities occurred much earlier, but they had been viewed as exceptions, rather than as the start of a new form. This new urban complex, economically united but politically divided, was seen as inefficient and ineffective. The new decentralized arrangement emerged despite a variety of legal remedies available to prevent it.

Annexation was the original device for preventing fragmentation through the amalgamation of newly developing urban fringe areas into the core city proper. As a city grew in population, its boundaries were to be extended. The breakdown of annexation began as soon as a vehicle was invented enabling people to live in the remote fringe and work in the city. This suggests that the desire for escape was previously present but that the electric trolley was necessary to provide the means. Tracks were laid into the countryside, and tracts of land were developed at intervals along them. Streetcar or rail suburbs developed around all the Eastern and Midwestern cities of the late nineteenth century. In order to obtain legal power for providing municipal services, these fringe developments were incorporated as distinct municipal corporations. The automobile simply provided the vehicle which could fill in the spaces left inaccessible by the rail web and paved the way for another round of suburban incorporations. But even after the automobile became the prime mode of intraurban movement, continuous and contiguous development was still rarely the norm. Developers leapfrogged over nearby vacant land to find cheaper land beyond. Thus, annexation has been continually frustrated by noncontiguous development, but other factors have undoubtedly been more basic in breaking down annexation as an integrating device. Social value conflicts and revenue-cost ratios strategies are undoubtedly among them. Fringe areas have resisted being "engulfed," particularly where core cities are lower in status,[1] and core cities have been reluctant to annex areas which will cost more to service than they will yield in revenue. Fringe areas which differ in status and wealth likewise rarely combine.

Some of the newer Western cities, having witnessed the consequences of fragmentation, have pursued a very aggressive annexation policy, which tries to extend core city boundaries ahead of growth. Many of the cities have annexed enormous stretches of bordering land within the last decade. However, as Table 1 indicates, not all those cities which were most aggressive in annexing their hinterland were able to prevent the formation of new cities around their periphery. Most of these new incorporated suburbs had small populations in 1960, but they represent substantial efforts to create islands of municipal dissent, which are likely to be permanent and to grow. Thus, the urge to decentralize seems present even where centralization is the official metropolitan policy.

Once there are a substantial number of contiguous incorporations, annexation is of little use in bringing about metropolitan government. An alternative is consolidation, or merging the many contiguous muncipalities into one. This sometimes takes the form of city-county consolidation proposals, in which the county re-

[1] Support is given this hypothesis by Thomas R. Dye, "Urban Political Integration: Conditions Associated with Annexation in American Cities," *Midwest Journal of Political Science* 8 (November 1964), p. 445.

Table 1
The Leaders in Annexation, 1950–1960, among Cities with 1960 Populations of 100,000 or More and SMSA New Incorporations

	Population	Land Area (square miles)		Land Increase 1950–1960	New Incorporations in SMSA's 1950–1960
		1950	1960		
Oklahoma City, Okla.	324,253	50.8	321.5	270.7	10
Phoenix, Ariz.	429,170	17.1	187.4	170.3	3
Houston, Tex.	938,219	160.0	328.1	168.1	9
Dallas, Tex.	679,684	112.0	279.9	167.9	18
Mobile, Ala.	202,779	25.4	152.9	127.5	4
San Diego, Calif.	573,224	99.4	192.4	93.0	3
Atlanta, Ga.	487,455	36.9	128.2	91.3	3
San Antonio, Tex	587,718	69.5	160.5	91.0	7
El Paso, Tex.	276,687	25.6	114.6	89.0	3
Newport News, Va.	113,662	4.2	75.0	70.8	1
Tampa, Fla.	274,970	19.0	85.0	66.0	6
Tucson, Ariz.	212,892	9.5	70.9	61.4	0
Lubbock, Tex.	128,691	17.0	75.0	58.0	2
Columbus, Ohio	471,316	39.4	89.0	49.6	1
Kansas City, Mo.	475,539	80.6	129.8	49.2	10
Fort Worth, Tex.	356,268	93.7	140.5	46.8	17
Milwaukee, Wisc.	741,324	50.0	91.1	41.1	14
Beaumont, Tex.	119,175	31.4	70.8	39.4	4
San Jose, Calif.	204,196	17.0	54.5	37.5	7

Source: Data developed from Bollens and Schmandt, op. cit., p. 412, and Richard Stauber, New Cities in America (1965).

places all the cities within its boundaries and becomes a city itself. Such proposals generally fail. Because it is difficult to enumerate failures or abortive attempts, an exact success-failure ratio cannot be established. However, there is probably no metropolitan area in the country in which there have not been several efforts to start metropolitan consolidation,[2] and if we confine ourselves to the most concerted attempts—those which moved the idea along to the point where some official body made a decision—we can come up with an approximate fail-success ratio. Prior to World War II, there were fourteen such attempts[3] and only one partial success—Baton Rouge, Louisiana—which approved a partial con-

[2] Between 1923 and 1957 there were 112 general metropolitan surveys published and numerous other special ones. See Robert O. Warren, *Governments in Metropolitan Regions: A Reappraisal of Fractionated Political Organization* (1966), p. 24.

[3] John C. Bollens and Henry J. Schmandt, *The Metropolis* (1965), pp. 429–430.

solidation plan under unique circumstances.[4] There were another twelve failures at city-county consolidations in the post World War II period listed by Bollens and Schmandt in 1963.[5] Since then, there have been other failures, but also three consolidations: Davidson County–Nashville, Tennessee; Jacksonville; and Duval County, Florida; and recently a legislatively imposed merger of Indianapolis and Marion County, Indiana.[6]

There have been several other types of metropolitan government attempted. One involves a federation of local governments, in which some powers are centralized and some are retained by constituent municipalities. One halfway federation was formed in Dade County, Florida. Another plan calls for transfers of functions from city to county governments. This is a piecemeal kind of arrangement, which usually envisions complete consolidation, but on a one service at a time basis. Some transfers have taken place, but comprehensive consolidation has never happened in this way.

Thus, after four decades of self-conscious promotion of the metropolitan idea, five or six metropolitan areas have achieved some kind of general governmental centralization through consolidation, and another half dozen or so (mostly in Texas) have reduced fragmentation by anticipatory annexation programs.[7] During the same span of time, many more metropolitan areas have come into being as formally fragmented and decentralized urban complexes. (Between 1963 and 1968 the number of SMSA's increased from 212 to 233.) Most of those that have been in existence continue to become governmentally more complicated, as

[4] See William C. Havard, Jr., and Floyd L. Corty, *Rural-Urban Consolidation* (1964). The metropolitan charter commission was set up by the voters of the state. The new quasi-consolidated government, which was finally approved, required only a single parish-wide majority vote for approval. Most consolidation plans require majorities in each jurisdiction being consolidated. The charter made a number of structural concessions to specific areas, including permanent tax concessions to industry. This was the closest thing to a state-imposed settlement on any metropolitan area in American experience.
[5] Bollens and Schmandt, *op. cit.*, pp. 432–433.
[6] In the latter two cases, a number of existing incorporated suburbs were left undisturbed, so the effect was to incorporate all unincorporated fringe areas into the core city.
[7] One state, Virginia, has long had a policy opposing metropolitan governmental fragmentation. It has been successful mostly in smaller metropolitan areas, less so in the larger ones.

Metropolitan Political Analysis

new municipalities are created each year on the fringe to accommodate part of the increased population. Table 2 gives some indication of the rate.

Table 2
Number of Municipal Incorporations Annually, 1950–1960*

Incorporation Date	Within SMSA's	Outside SMSA's	Total
1950–51	48	40	88
1951–52	41	55	96
1952–53	35	57	92
1953–54	48	55	103
1954–55	42	43	85
1955–56	63	68	131
1956–57	69	52	121
1957–58	65	43	108
1958–59	49	53	102
1959–60	81	63	144
Unknown	1	3	4
Total	542	532	1,074

* Year—April 1 to March 31.
Source: Stauber, op. cit., p. 3.

The possibility of metropolitan government becomes even more bleak if one considers the changes in the nature of urban complexes. The metropolitan government movement conceived the metropolitan area as a core city surrounded by suburbs. Metropolitan government meant joining the core and the ring into one government. However, it is now quite apparent that huge urban areas are emerging which have no core or ring. They are simply shapeless, spreading urban conglomerations. This trend has often welded two or three preexisting old metropolitan areas into a single urban mass. From the foregoing, it is fairly obvious that the forty-year effort to bring about metropolitan consolidation will not end in success. This is the case even though the metropolitan integration appeal was based on *equity* and *economy,* and the arguments sound persuasive. The economy argument talks about the scale of municipal enterprises. While the optimum size of a city cannot be definitely established,[8] from what we *do* know, many existing municipalities are too small to

[8] Otis Dudley Duncan, "The Optimum Size of Cities," in Paul K. Hatt and Albert J. Reiss (eds.), *Cities and Society* (1957), pp. 759–772.

be efficient. Certainly, water and sewage treatment systems are more efficient on a large scale. The multiplication of building codes may impede mass production of housing. Small cities have difficulty maintaining technical training facilities for employees. Public health people argue that a minimum number of employees in a local health staff is necessary to assure the needed mix of skills to staff an adequate program. Though the professionals in each service system would draw different boundaries in defining an ideal service area, few would choose the present metropolitan form of decentralization.

The equity argument of the integrationists is even more cogent. It asserts that decentralization segregates resources for meeting problems from the responsibility for solving them. While social problems are generated by the whole urban complex, they often manifest themselves in discreet areas or municipalities. The tax resources to cope with these problems are unlikely to exist in the same municipalities which must foot the bill for solutions. While the poor, the industrial cripple, and the dropout are clustered spatially, the conditions which produce them are more general. While the place lottery of the property tax brings revenue largess to the municipality which is the home of the factory, the municipality where the worker lives foots the school bill with meagre resources. Not only finances and problems are segregated, but other resources as well. James Madison argued in the *Federalist Papers* that since leadership is not randomly distributed spatially, small areas are often wanting in this respect. If this is the case, the present metropolitan order may have inequitably distributed leadership resources, so that some municipalities suffer from a lack of interested civic talent. Thus, the equity argument is one which advocates a pooling of problems and resources by creating larger units of urban local government.

While many structural changes overtly are in response to these equity and economy arguments, they have been made in nearly every conceivable way except through metropolitan government. There have been state mandated tax rebates, shared taxes, and grants-in-aid. There have been many local government adjustments and changes, including special districts, functional transfers to county governments, cooperative arrangements, and jointures. The question is: Why has there been such widespread resistance to creating larger general-purpose units of local government, and how do we explain the particular arrangements which have emerged?

Style Specialization

It is axiomatic that specialization and interdependence are complementary processes. We have argued that metropolitan areas are characterized by spatial specialization. The distribution which emerges could not exist without linkages between the divergent areas. The existence of a wealthy residential suburb presumes also a variety of working-class and middle-class residential areas nearby. Differing levels of wealth and status are functions of a common economic and social system. In order for the various occupational groups and social classes to exist, they must interact through sociospatial units which involve nonfamily roles. These mixing units and mixing areas must be linked together, and they must draw on common urban infrastructures. The maintenance of areal specialization requires communication, transportation, and other infrastructure systems.

The massive tie-ups on expressways, the increased sales of automobiles, the technological emphasis on communication hardware all testify to the great demand for linkages, exchanges, and interactions. Common facilities, such as airports, wharves, museums, universities, and stadiums, must exist somewhere in a metropolitan area. Common air and watersheds more than symbolize interdependencies; their pollution links interdependence and existence.

The need for rationalizing services which facilitate interactions, added to the considerations of equity and economy, would seem to provide yet another reason for political integration in metropolitan areas. Because the proposals for metropolitan government seemed reasonable, early efforts to explain the record of failures stressed citizen ignorance. It was argued that if only citizens were better informed they would vote for metropolitan government. This logic led, in some metropolitan areas, to intensive educational campaigns. However, in metropolitan areas, such as St. Louis and Cleveland, substantial information campaigns seemed to have little positive effect on gaining voting support for metropolitan government. They may even have had adverse effects.

Political scientists have made a number of attempts to explain why metropolitan integration has failed or, in a few cases, succeeded. A number of studies have used a case approach.[9] Unfortunately, most case studies inevitably lead to a list of particular interests which came forward in particular situations and did battle; it is impossible to add up case studies into any theory of metropolitan behavior. Both Holden[10] and Toscano[11] have tried to build more systematically on the surmises of the municipal reformers who pleaded for more informed publics. Holden asserts spatial communities inevitably become isolated and can best be understood in terms of interacting sovereign entities. Thus, he sees a metropolitan area behaving something like the international system. His reasoning by analogy is only suggestive. Toscano tried to supply more evidence. He raised the question of whether rewarding interaction experience between municipalities breaks down barriers, thus leading to greater and greater cooperation. If municipalities are, indeed, like nation-states and if their separateness impedes knowledge of one another, then when mutually beneficial communication does occur, increased communication, cooperation, and integration should result. However, using empirical data, he found that this cumulative "spill over" affect from one favorable experience to another was not supported.

The problem with the spill over hypothesis is that separateness is not tantamount to lack of mutual understanding and knowledge among units in the metropolitan area. Completely the opposite is more likely the case. Separation is derived from very good reciprocal information and knowledge. Unlike the international situation, there is a relatively free flow of population. The

[9] Examples include Edward Sofen, *The Miami Metropolitan Experiment* (1963); Winston W. Crouch and Beatrice Dinerman, *Southern California Metropolis* (1963); Henry J. Schmandt and William H. Standing, *The Milwaukee Metropolitan Study Commission* (1965); William C. Havard and Floyd L. Corty, *Rural-Urban Consolidation* (1964); David A. Booth, *Metropolitics: The Nashville Consolidation* (1963).

[10] Mathew Holden, Jr., "The Governance of the Metropolis as a Problem in Diplomacy," *Journal of Politics*, 26 (August 1964), pp. 627–647.

[11] James V. Toscano, "Transaction Flow Analysis in Metropolitan Areas: Some Preliminary Explorations," in Philip E. Jacob and James V. Toscano (eds.), *The Integration of Political Communities* (1964), pp. 111–119.

separateness and differences among communities is a function of many locational choices and sets of coalitional actions, and not simply a legacy or accident of history. Increased information may indeed be dysfunctional to any effort to achieve overall political integration. Better information may serve to underline the basic cleavages that exist.

Let us now draw upon the social access notion of urbanism and use it to explain centralizing and decentralizing tendencies. That which must be examined is not simply the failure of complete, metropolitan-wide governments to emerge, but also the decisions to centralize or decentralize along functional lines. In order to explain these two tendencies, a twofold classification of urban policies will be used. This classification, which has been elsewhere presented by the author, divides urban policies into those which involve a direct expression of preferred interactions and those which generally facilitate the choice of interactions. The former have been called *life style* policies and the latter *system maintenance* policies.[12]

The life style concept is used because it connotes a value cluster associated with a daily living pattern. It is a complex set of preferences pertaining to the frequency, character, and context of interactions. The concept goes beyond the usual demographic or ecological description of clusterings of objective characteristics of the sociospatial units or their members. Objective attributes may or may not be good indicators of distinct styles. Whether there is a correlation between social class and life styles is an empirical question. However, if members of a social class *do* cluster spatially, it is not because they are of the same social class, but rather because of certain values (life style) which make interaction along class lines rewarding.

Life style is intended to be a very inclusive term, which denotes the social access policy of any sociospatial unit, including households, factories, offices, stores, and churches. We are, of course, primarily interested here in those social access policies which are place contingent. For example, Greer speaks of indi-

[12] Oliver P. Williams, "Life Style Values and Political Decentralization in Metropolitan Areas," *Southwestern Social Science Quarterly*, 48 (December 1967), pp. 299–310.

viduals as being *neighbors, community actors and isolates,* according to the intensity of their intraurban interaction patterns.[13] While ostensibly every manufacturing firm seeks to maximize profits, the way it goes about this has an urban style manifestation. For example, a decision to rely on cheap labor, rather than to automate, will affect the firm's access needs and hence its location.

Certain urban policies directly involve critical interactions associated with life style, while others are neutral in this regard. A prime example of the former is education. Educational policy in our urban language defines who will come together in a sociospatial unit called a school. The membership (pupils, teachers, and staff) in the school is determined by attendance area designations, hiring policies, levels of support, and curriculum structure. Zoning or land use policies are similarly life style policies in that they place limits on who is likely to interact with whom and in what role capacity the interactions will take place.

Zoning and schools are two prime local policy areas which affect the socialization of children and the casual associations centered around the domicile. To a lesser extent, other civic policies, such as those which pertain to libraries, recreation programs, cultural programs, and certain aspects of police and health programs, also partake of these qualities. The life style effects of these services often manifest themselves in subtle ways. The city recreation director must have the right attitude toward organized "little leagues." The police department will exhibit various styles of law enforcement in response to community characteristics.[14] Local librarians may or may not be expected to organize Saturday morning story hours. Home maternity visits by a public health nurse may be insulting to the well-doctored middle class, but socially acceptable in a working-class area. Even garbage and trash collection have their style nuance—backdoor collection for the rich; cheaper, street side collection for the lower middle class. Because of a peculiar American tradition, fire departments may, at times, also be added to the list. In many areas, volunteer departments are more community social organizations than fire

---

[13] Scott Greer, *The Emerging City* (1962), p. 120.
[14] James Q. Wilson, *Varieties of Police Behavior* (1968).

fighting groups. Historically, internal loyalties within fire fighting companies have been unusually intense and constant impediments to structural reorganization.

The system maintenance policies are perceived as neutral with regard to life style values. They are those services which are necessary to make the system of specialized areas work. They facilitate choices of interactions rather than structure them. The most obvious example is the transportation network. It was the development of integrated transportation networks which made great daily mobility within the metropolis possible and the consequent spatial segregation of roles and styles. Because of this fact, formerly the rails and now the highways are all important organizers of urban space. Locations are structured with respect to the networks. Electronic communication networks are also system maintenance services. Because access to these networks has little to do with location, urban man is now freed from locational dependencies in many areas of his life, representing a marked change in urban organization. A whole range of considerations in locational choices has been removed by the electronic revolution. Interestingly, in nations where telephones and television are in short supply, locational choices are often made which enable tapping into these systems, in much the same way that an American sociospatial unit locates near an expressway interchange.

Wharves, airports, mass transit, port facilities, trade centers, and stadiums are among the publicly provided, specialized receptacles for facilitating interactions; they, too, are essential for maintaining the system. Similarly, water, sewerage, and other utilities fall in the system maintenance class, because they enable the system of area specialization to grow and thrive.

System maintenance functions are not politically vacuous; they do give rise to controversy. In considering such controversies, it is important to distinguish between normal political issues and those which are particularly urban. For example, cost is always a source of conflict in all political arenas. Any change in a service usually involves the need for some new revenue. Opportunities for discrimination or differential treatment are endless in revenue policies, which can cause unlimited friction. Revenue increases are examples of *normal* political questions. Changes in system maintenance facilities involve peculiarly *urban* issues when social access patterns are affected. Even a sewage disposal plant can, under certain circumstances, be the focal point of a highly political issue in the urban sense. That is, a new sewage treatment plant can affect who is going to be accessible to whom. A brief illustration will demonstrate this point.

Land varies as to its percolation qualities, that is, its ability to absorb liquids. Thus, land parcels vary as to housing densities they can safely tolerate with individual, on-site sewage disposal systems. Areas with poor percolation might require densities of one- to even five-acre minimum lot sizes. However, a public sewage plant renders irrelevant this rationale for low density, making intensive development feasible from a health standpoint. As housing density is associated with life styles, ultimately the type of sewage system may affect just who is going to live next to whom. Sewage treatment plants have been opposed as indirect efforts to maintain low housing densities.

If we have areal specialization, it follows that life style policies are likely to be decentralized. As there is no complete consensus on the salience of all life style policies, some groups or localities may be less concerned about a particular policy area than another; therefore, some bargaining on particular services is possible. But proposals for general governmental integration will be vehemently opposed because they touch salient life style concerns of many different groups.

For areal specialization to exist, there must be some area-wide services; that is, there must be some overall system maintaining structures. These services or structures are more likely to be centrally planned, financed, or controlled. However, policy changes which are system maintaining for the overall metropolitan area may completely transform the life style of a particular area. A freeway network may serve areal specialization in general and therefore receive diffuse support from the metropolitan area. A locality which absorbs the impact of a major expressway interchange within its boundaries is likely to fight vehemently for local veto powers, for its life style may be threatened. System maintenance services often pit area-wide interests against specific local interests, with the former usually prevailing in the long run.

A survey of metropolitan reorganization patterns would seem to give credence to the dichotomy between life style and system maintenance policies. It is especially instructive to look at the Miami–Dade County experience. While Metropolitan Dade County represents one of the few successfully created general area-wide governments, the pattern of conflict during its formation parallels the dichotomy. The Metro charter gave sweeping powers to the overall government. But when the specific ordinances were introduced to transfer power from existing municipalities to the new government, the articulation of local claims became vociferous. The effort to centralize zoning and building inspection was defeated.[15] While this was the only substantial victory for the municipalities, other hard and bitter fights occurred over local control of traffic enforcement, licensing, and regulatory powers generally. Not surprisingly, the municipality which fought hardest against Metro was Miami Beach, the unit with the most distinctive characteristics.[16]

Following several rejections of comprehensive area-wide government, St. Louis metropolitan citizens approved special districts for transportation facilities and sewage disposal. Seattle went through a similar experience. The major examples of metropolitan-wide special districts are transit-transportation related and utilities.[17] Many other similar examples can be noted. Among the area-wide special districts the major exception to the dichotomy seems to be parks. There are three or four metropolitan park districts. However, all were created in the early part of the century, prior to the automobile era. Park authorities were primarily designed to buy rural land outside the incorporated areas. It is very doubtful that similar area-wide park authorities could be created today in any of the larger metropolitan areas.

A perusal of the issues of *Metropolitan Area Digest* over the past few years gives a picture of present trends in structural changes. The big rage is for councils of local governments. These are conferences of elected officials from local governments, who meet together to discuss and plan for the solution of common area-based problems. Action is usually contingent on unanimous agreement, as most councils have no legal power to act. Such

[15] Edward Sofen, *op. cit.*, pp. 122–124.
[16] *Ibid.*, pp. 90–91, 124–127, 161–162.
[17] John C. Bollens, *Special District Governments in the United States* (1957), chap. 2.

councils now are officially recognized in federal law as meeting requirements for metropolitan planning in various conditional grant statutes. The councils vary greatly in effectiveness, but they can be no stronger than the voluntarism of local areas will allow.

Aside from the actions of councils, one gathers from the *Digest* that there are very few structural changes occurring in metropolitan areas of an area-wide nature, though the studies which investigate proposals for basic changes continue to be numerous. Perhaps the most significant developments are the planning and financing of metropolitan transportation programs by state and regional governments.

While few substantial changes have taken place in evolving centralized structures, an ingenious plan for decentralization has been developed. The Lakewood Plan, which is named for the innovating city, involves suburban incorporation followed by contracting for all municipal services from the county. In the Lakewood case, Los Angeles County was already in the urban service business on a large scale, and it could provide services more cheaply than a small city could for itself. The Lakewood Plan eliminates the efficiency and economy argument against decentralization, but it does nothing about the equity argument. The plan only works where there is a county government willing and able to perform the services. These "instant cities" can tailor their life style policies even more flexibly than normal suburbs and have the advantages of large-scale economies at the same time.

Most of this descriptive evidence supports the following propositions as constituting the metropolitan political "settlement." *Assuming no outside interventions, policy areas which are perceived as neutral with respect to controlling social access may be centralized; policies which are perceived as controlling social access will remain decentralized.* Outside intervention could, of course, abridge these metropolitan tendencies, and we will now consider them.

Intergovernmental Relations

Local governments do not operate autonomously. Their legal powers are granted by state governments. In certain respects, local governments are administrative units of the state, and even federal, government. Local governments receive conditional grants and shared revenues from higher levels. Various agencies at the state and federal level form concrete strategies specifically designed to influence local policies. Consequently, although there is a tradition of local self-government generally in the American states, there are many interventions from "above." What is the influence of such interventions on the metropolitan political "settlement?"

In this area, the evidence is sparse, and even surmises are hazardous. It is evident that if the metropolitan "settlement" is to be abridged by society, intervention must come from some jurisdiction larger than that controlled by the actors in a specific urban complex. Other nations have chosen this path; many European countries have, for a long time, treated urban development patterns as matters of national concern. There, access allocation is more a function of national political party and ideological interplay than of the working out of an ecological or local bargaining process. The level at which control over the urban process is placed can have a dramatic effect. This question should be high on the agenda of an as yet undeveloped area of specialization in comparative urban politics.

Nations which undertake the responsibility for building new towns inevitably lay bare the town-creating process. When towns are self-consciously created, it suddenly becomes clear where the urban policy decisions lie. Questions which are treated as if they are a matter of God's will or the eternal verities in the United States are seen to be matters of choice controlled by man's actions. The result of nationalizing concern over urban development is to convert decisions from the private domain of social processes to the public domain of political activity. Compared with European experience, intergovernmental intervention has not radically altered the urban process in the United States. Despite the great and widespread concern with cities and the plethora of federally funded urban programs, there is some question about the impact of this recent attention, to say nothing of the past decisions.

The federal government has often used the conditional grant as a major means of influencing policies at lower levels. There are a very large number of federal grants-in-aid programs to local areas. Those which include conditions requiring some regional planning are highways, mass transit, and airports. The other, older and large, federal urban subsidy programs are public housing and urban renewal. In both of these cases, regional planning is not required, and local control is assured. Both have implications for changing local life styles and interaction patterns. Thus, the federal government fits into the ongoing way of doing business in metropolitan areas. Even though a good case could be made for the metropolitan-wide treatment of all these services, it is only required for the system maintenance functions. Low-cost housing is not coordinated with either sources of employment or transportation routes to employment. No recognition is given to the fact that low-income people are part of a metropolitan complex, not simply residents of a municipality, unlucky enough to have a stock of filtered-down houses. Regional effects of urban renewal are not really recognized in that program.

The federal programs which structurally can have substantial effects on the urban process are those which channel aid directly to individuals. Aid in the form of welfare payments or rent subsidies increases individual mobility. By redistributing resources directly to individuals, rather than to municipalities, the capacity of welfare recipients to make favorable ecological adaptations to the urban milieu is, indeed, enhanced. However, welfare payments have never been substantial, and subsistence is their general object. Thus, direct welfare payments have done relatively little to equalize mobility opportunities. In fact, the programs of direct benefits to individuals with the greatest impact on urban areas are guaranteed mortgages and income tax deduction policies. These policies have financed the creation of suburbs and have underwritten the new areas of residential spatial specialization of the past several decades.

States have less frequently engaged in conditional grants than in shared taxes as a means of intervening in metropolitan areas. The equalizing grants have done much to blunt the harsh impact of metropolitan decentralization on the poorer local jurisdictions. The question is: Do shared revenues make the decentralized metropolis possible and dampen moves for consolidation?

If one looks at the distribution of tax bases across any metropolitan area by municipality or school district, it is apparent that jurisdictions share property wealth unevenly. Some suburbs combine small populations with large industrial complexes; small and dense residential areas may be incorporated without any nonresidential property; and a variety of other combinations will lie in between. Many of the poorest suburban school districts would never have been able to open schools if they had had to remain completely dependent on their own revenues. The political pressure of impoverished school districts faced states with two alternatives. Districts would have had to be consolidated in order to pool wealth, or the state would have had to subsidize the poor ones. Inequities among rural districts, combined with the suburban situation, created a political climate in which most states opted for the latter course.

Throughout the fifty states, there are many different patterns of state aid to schools and municipalities. There is no state that does not transfer some funds to local governments, though New Jersey strenuously tried not to for many years. Generally, the effect of state policies is to remove the extreme financial curse of metropolitan decentralization. It should be noted that such a subsidy system does not radically disturb the metropolitan "settlement." It does not substantially affect the question of who will be accessible to whom. Intergovernmental transfer and shared taxes ostensibly only place a service floor below which local services cannot fail. But in some states these revenue transfer arrangements have been the object of manipulation. Each local area works for criteria which favor jurisdictions with its particular characteristics. The municipalities with superior political resources often get favored treatment.

In brief, while state and federal governments have been greatly concerned with urban problems, the relationship between these levels and the local jurisdictions is such that substantial changes in urban access patterns are unlikely to come from intergovernmental programs. Indeed, the existing metropolitan settlement is made financially possible by state and federal urban policies.

Chapter 7

THE
METROPOLITAN
SETTLEMENT
AND
THE
FUTURE

There is every likelihood that in the future most Americans will live in metropolitan areas. While a few new population centers will be created, for the most part increases in urban population will be accommodated at the periphery of existing urban complexes. For this reason, it is worth asking what the implications are of continuing the "metropolitan settlement." What is likely to be the result of a national policy which stresses the individual entrepreneurial role in city formation and uses central planning in a parsimonious and restricted fashion? Which values are most served and which least?

Dimensions of Spatial Specialization

Every city or urban center is characterized by some pattern of spatial articulation. The interesting thing about the American metropolis is that spatially specialized areas become legal jurisdictions, fully equipped with powers of self-government. Examples of highly specialized municipalities serve to dramatize the result of giving political, as well as social, meaning to segments of urban space. The most striking occur, interestingly, in new urban areas, where the possibilities of municipal specialization have been most fully explored. The cities of Industry and Commerce in southern California have been created for the purposes their names symbolize. They were incorporated to keep people out (residential land use, that is) and to provide a local environment and set of policies strictly for business. Dairy Valley and Walnut are interesting "antiurban" cities. In each case, high value dairy farming areas were incorporated in order to gain zoning power and thereby exclude encroachment of urban land uses. Irwindale was incorporated as a quarrying and rock crushing area. Its inhabitants consist mainly of a small Mexican-American colony, but the purpose of the incorporation was to protect quarrying interests against municipal regulation.[1] Sometimes suburbs assume specialized functions in relationship to the entire metropolitan area. A commonplace type has been the vice suburb, which supplies a kind of entertainment considered illicit in other parts of the urban complex, but for which there is a great demand. More legitimate kinds of entertainment are supplied by ocean or park fronting suburbs. Other common servicing suburbs offer industrial parks with high performance standards or industrial areas where no questions will be asked.

Most suburbs do not pursue such singular strategies. Their kind of specialization tends to grow out of the accretion of individual choices. The result is that most metropolitan municipalities move toward some type of relative specialization by embracing only a certain range of the population, according to any dimension. There is a place for the young, the old, the rich, the poor, the Catholic, the bigoted, and the broadminded. There hardly exists a municipality which is a true sample of the greater metropolitan area.

Considered in one sense, this suburban municipal specialization connotes the image of something that is very much in keeping with hallowed American beliefs. It suggests pluralism, choice, an opportunity for like-minded people to band together to form a community. Community formation, whether on the Western or suburban frontier, seems to be a form of democratic participation. When people find their needs are not met by existing local government arrangements, they can exercise initiative and create something closer to their liking.

Does the result lead simply to the benefit of the enterprising few, or can it be argued that decentralization works for the bene-

[1] Robert D. Warren, *Government in Metropolitan Regions: A Reappraisal of Fractionated Political Organization* (1966), chap. 10.

fit of all? It is my belief that the former is the case, but there is one interesting defense of community specialization along social class lines. The logic of this argument begins with the assumption that working-class populations are not socialized into politics the way middle-class populations are. It is Gans's claim that the whole organizational, committee-forming, mutual subordinating process is very much middle class.[2] As a result, despite their numerical strength, working-class populations usually come out second best in political contests with the middle class. Middle-class populations can outmaneuver, outorganize, and outlast lower class groups. If metropolitan decentralization segregates along class lines, as it appears, this should protect working-class populations from the dangers of the middle-class takeover. At the same time, the middle-class populations can practice their organizational skills on one another in their own bailiwicks.

The American metropolis caters not simply to class, but also to industry, farmers, vice lords, and religious groups; indeed, any group with sufficient enterprise can create its own little community. The decentralized system seems to offer to many what they want, and because it can cope with such diversity, it is a very popular political form.

Cramps in the System and System Responses

As the metropolitan reform movement clearly indicates, the decentralized system of governing metropolitan areas fails to satisfy some. Proposals for metropolitan government, however inadequately supported, have not been fabricated completely from textbooks. There are certain cramps in the system which manifest themselves in ways other than proposals for reform.

One could pick any of a whole range of problems to illustrate some of the consequences of our present urban strategy. I have selected four urban policy matters with which every large city in history has had to deal. All large cities must create some means for internal circulation; they must dispose of waste products; they

---

[2] Gans, *The Urban Villager* (1962). Gans documents class difference in political behavior. He does not advocate separate local political units of a class character.

must deal with physical obsolescence; and they must provide for population increases.

1. *Circulation.* How well do we attend to the problems of internal circulation within the metropolis? This is difficult to answer in any absolute sense. Traffic jams, commuting times, and hours spent in travel give some justification for saying not well enough. But such statements are only assertive. Let us consider for the moment only the logic of a solution. It is quite clear that transportation is a *system;* hence, it must be planned for in a systematic fashion. All metropolitan areas, however zealously they guard local prerogatives, have had to concede, at least in principal, the need for some central planning in transportation. However this need not mean overall planning for all the various circulation systems. Clear choices among transportation systems are made. Furthermore, as all traffic engineers know only too well, an integral part of transportation planning is the control of trip generation, and control over this area is never centralized.

There are few examples of truly regional transportation planning and effectuating agencies in the United States, ones which integrate highway, rail, air, bus, and new hardware systems. Most transportation agencies have truncated and partial jurisdictions. There are no systems which tie together land development planning and control with transportation policies.

Highways are more conducive than rails to the formation of spatially specialized retreats. The rigidity of rail networks reduces the combinations of locational options open to individuals. The use of separate urban spaces for various roles stresses the need for flexible mobility. The automobile seems the better tool for extremes of spatial specialization. Rail systems require fixed points of convergence, and the range of entrepreneurial choice is drastically reduced for developing new areas.

The specialized suburb and the highway-based circulation system go hand in hand. However, such a circulation policy would have severe direct adverse consequences for part of the population. In order for this kind of system to work for all, there must be universal automobile ownership. This would create a real problem for the many who cannot drive an automobile for reasons of age or health or, more significantly, cannot afford one or can do so only with great financial difficulty. To a poor person, dependent on public transportation for access to a job, the present auto-oriented circulation policy is a disaster. Bus service in the suburbs is terrible, and rapid transit lines are not being generally extended. Fares for public transit are rising more rapidly than the cost of auto travel. Jobs are rapidly being decentralized away from the core areas having public transportation. The usual strategy for employees caught in these circumstances is to shorten their trip; in other words, they move closer to the job. But the land use control system prevents this from working. Low-cost housing is not following the dispersal pattern of jobs.[3] Suburbs which welcome factories often exclude housing in the price range which industrial workers, particularly those in lower paying jobs, can afford. Blacks are excluded by a variety of devices. Public housing in the suburbs is nearly unheard of. Jobs are being placed literally out of reach of the poor.

Thus, while the circulation system is planned on a system-wide basis, the effective demand for great spatial specialization gives strong support to the priority of an expensive automobile highway system.

2. *Removal of waste.* If cities fail to realize that all of their inhabitants, as well as sociospatial units, not only consume but also discharge, then suddenly they find themselves mired in their own filth. The scale of an urban place is directly related to the rapidity with which this is likely to take place. The linkage between the growth of urbanism and the deterioration of the environmental quality has recently been realized in this country. However, man has a long history of failure in cities in dealing with environmental pollution, as those who have read Lewis Mumford are well aware.[4] Indeed disease stemming from environmental contamination has been a major factor limiting urban growth at various times in history.

When the cities of antiquity were small, they had many internal open spaces, and night soil was planted in the gardens. When social access demands heightened, densities increased and gar-

---

[3] For accounts of unemployment and job decentralization, see the *Monthly Labor Review.* Articles on the subject appear throughout 1967 issues.

[4] Lewis Mumford, *The City in History* (1961), pp. 214–218.

dens were built over. The result was environmental contamination of the worst order. All roads led to Rome where the action was, populations crowded into this capital center and the waste disposal problems of that city of antiquity became enormous. The city responded with prodigious efforts. The very scale of the catacombs and the Cloaca Maxima dramatize the severity of the problem they faced. The Romans recognized that the problem required a massive and well-coordinated response. In the end, however, the task proved too much for them and environmental health deteriorated to a very low level. We find ourselves in an analogous situation today.

In the United States, environmental health has been traditionally a local matter. Historically health regulation was considered one of the residual police powers left to local governments under the Constitutional division of powers. Thus, local health departments are a result of legal views concerning the areal division of power. The survival of this arrangement which makes health a local matter is largely fortuitous. Just at the time when American cities began to grow rapidly and increase in density, medical technology began to control communicable disease through vaccination and immunization. The general public also became better educated in matters of personal hygiene. The local health officers contributed some by checking on cesspools, wells and eating establishments, but their role in making cities livable was largely supplementary.

Today we face a new environmental health problem, not of communicable diseases, but one stemming from the deterioration of the general environment. The exponential growth of industrial production is releasing enormous quantities of waste into the environment. Local municipalities are still the legal bodies assigned the responsibility for doing something about this problem. What is more ludicrous than holding municipalities in a metropolitan area responsible for air pollution abatement? How can one expect a small municipality to crack down on its major industry and taxpayer so that residents on the windward side in a different municipality will breathe less polluted air? Similarly, consider and contrast the massive distribution industry, which daily brings enormous quantities of consumption goods into every large urban complex, with the local trash men who are supposed to dispose of the resulting residue. Solid waste disposal remains largely a local responsibility and it is one of the most technologically backward industries in the nation. It is also one in which there is very little investment in research by the operators, who are, of course, largely municipal governments.

One of the byproducts of the metropolitan settlement has been this hiatus between the large-scale nature of urban environmental pollution problems and the small capacity of local governments to handle them.

3. *Obsolescence.* Physical obsolescence of cities is not new. Cities have been aging for centuries and programs of urban renewal have recurred throughout history. We referred in Chapter 1 to the urban renewal projects of the Hellenist period and of nineteenth-century Paris. In ages when the public-private dichotomy of capitalist cultures was less pronounced, urban renewal was very much an affair of state. While we have rebuilt most of our older American cities several times over, it is only recently that public subsidies have become required. Formerly, ghost towns developed, with private citizens absorbing the losses, or increased density demands in the city core areas allowed speculative capital to tear down and rebuild, and still make a profit. At the end of the coke-steam technological era, private investment interest in core area renewal declined, as outlying areas became more attractive alternatives for industry.

Federal urban renewal legislation, as originally written, conceived the problem as a breakdown in private redevelopment. In addition, slums were viewed as bad spots on an apple. If the spots could be eliminated, they would not spread, and the city would return to health. For this, subsidies were called upon to bring private redevelopment back to the core. Of course, the conception proved faulty, and we have been groping from one strategy to another ever since. The demolition aspects of urban renewal rightfully identified a need to shift physical urban space from a nineteenth- to a twentieth-century organization. The patterns of access requirements today are indeed different from the time when the present cities were built. But renewal policies unwittingly got more than was bargained for because they have been projected into the center of a major social upheaval, which has little to do with buildings but much to do with access aspirations of black people. As a result, renewal policies began to shift away from demolition toward social programs.

The way in which both the original and the more recent policies of renewal are handled falls very much within the framework of the metropolitan settlement. Under federal urban renewal law, individual municipalities are largely responsible for initiating, local financing, and carrying through programs according to federally defined standards. Let us consider first what happens with physical renewal and second with social renewal.

The manifestations of physical obsolescence are not confined to the core cities. The nineteenth-century technological urban form exists not only in large central cities but also in many satellite cities scattered around the older major metropolitan centers, and in the core city of many smaller metropolitan areas. The result is that we have many entirely obsolete municipalities, not simply obsolete parts of cities. These obsolete satellites and small core cities are completely surrounded by later urban development, and now exist as grisly clumps of dysfunctional loft factory structures, rows of abandoned small commercial properties, old-style tenements, and business districts which are inaccessible to an automobile-oriented public. These cities have declining tax bases, as a succession of lower and lower wage firms occupy the cheap rental space. Underinvestment characterizes all aspects of civic and private life, leadership has moved away, and anger and frustration are the chief political commodities. How can physical urban renewal as presently constituted help these cities? Rarely is their location attractive for new uses, even if the land were cleared. Furthermore, clearance for a small municipality is self-annihilation and hence usually politically impossible. Some small metropolitan areas threaten to become donut-shaped with a hollow, vacated core city surrounded by a newer circle-shaped urban area. These places cannot engage in bootstraps operations, so that modern ghost towns are emerging in the very heart of urban areas. The ghosts which inhabit these twentieth-century versions are likely to be real people about whom the rest of society would just as soon forget.

The large core cities are in trouble, of course, but urban renewal still has some meaning for them. They do have leadership, resources, administrative skill, and, most important, locations which remain viable. The large cities can still construct some new major high density mix areas, which attract private investment. The basic notion of drawing resources from the good areas to correct the bad has meaning to a certain extent in Philadelphia, Chicago, Detroit, and San Francisco. It has much less meaning in New Bedford, Holyoke, Bayonne, Chester, and many smaller versions of them.

If we look upon renewal as a social rather than a physical rehabilitation program, the present decentralization of initiative and responsibility again reflects the metropolitan settlement. The ghetto is a classic illustration of the use of location as a strategy for delimiting access of a segment of the society. Ghetto dwellers are treated differently because they are ghetto dwellers. There is not a single large scale organization with scattered branches which does not develop special policies for its ghetto outlets. Each time a ghetto dweller taps into a large social structure, he is likely to be treated differently because of his address. The address is a badge, the first screening device for personal classification. The arresting policeman, the bill collector, the credit evaluator, the social worker, the school teacher, the municipal official, the insurance salesman all say, "Look where he lives." As long as black ghettoes were legally maintained, ghetto residency was easily structured and enforced. After the restrictive covenants were thrown out, blacks were able to increase their legal and political power in the core city, making neighborhood exclusion more difficult, and in most Northern large cities the walls of the ghetto were broken in the core cities, even though ghettoes themselves remained. Then a more ingenious device, metropolitan decentralization, came along. It is efficient in segregating people spatially along many subtle lines; it is excellent for sorting people by so obvious a characteristic as race.

One of the social properties of ghetto inhabitants is that they do not have the same opportunities as other urbanites for linking into all the social access relations that characterize urban life. Decentralization of authority for working on ghetto and obsolescence problems is a very good device for not working on them. For example, if a man is unemployed because he is excluded from all housing which is accessible to jobs, the only body which can attack the problem must comprehend jurisdictionally both the places of work and accessible residential areas.

Can we, within metropolitan areas, simply walk away and leave whole obsolete cities? Can we treat the obsolete physical areas imbedded in the midst of our metropolitan centers in the same way that we have treated ghost towns in the West? Can we continue to pursue a policy which fails to see that ghettoes, particularly black ghettoes, are in part products of the present metropolitan arrangement? Neither obsolete physical or social forms can be remedied in the metropolitan context through the present decentralization of responsibility.

4. *Growth.* The population curve in recent history has been upward in all nations, and except for some periods of severe pestilence and economic depression, urban populations have increased. At least until now, urbanization and industrialization have gone hand in hand. Although every nation has needed a policy for handling increased urban population, until quite recently few nations have had one. This does not mean, however, that the pattern of urban growth is unrelated to national policies. Decisions concerning transportation routes, natural resource development, trade subsidies, and tariffs all influence the location and distribution of cities. However, the way in which the growth question is faced frontally is in relation to city form, that is, city size, shape, density, and functional specialization.

We have not, as yet, been very self-conscious about this question in the United States. Nevertheless, national policies have, in fact, had great influence on the developing form of our cities. While we do not have a national policy on urban form *per se,* subsidies to middle-class home owners through tax laws and mortgage insurance, highway and rail policies, and the general acceptance of the metropolitan settlement are, in fact, form policies.

The self-conscious discussion about form has usually taken place among groups in separate metropolitan areas. Often the discussants are metropolitan planning and study councils. While regional highway and open space plans give some leverage toward actualizing a policy, the present metropolitan settlement nearly assures that everywhere our national policy for population increases will be accommodation through agglomeration and conurbanization. We will simply spread out in an inarticulated fashion from existing centers; newcomers and low-income people will crowd in and raise densities in some older areas. In the final analysis, the shape of the future is a function of private industrial location and development entrepreneur decisions. The private sector, expressing itself through individual sociospatial moves, largely shapes the new urban form.

The way we, as a nation, handle policy matters connected with circulation, waste removal, obsolescence, and growth is profoundly affected by our metropolitan political organization. Decentralization is biased to isolate problems, enabling them to be treated as local matters when they are not. In the case of pollution, this arrangement is at least now being questioned on a national basis. As for transportation, urban renewal, and urban form development, the metropolitan settlement seems very much intact. The interaction between the way we handle these problems and the resulting distribution of urban benefits is one of the important items on the agenda for future urban research.

The Future Research Agenda in Metropolitan Analysis

The foregoing set of social commentaries rests on a whole series of surmises about the present course of metropolitan development. The aim is to focus the attention of political science on a process which needs study but which is now largely ignored. The assertions may be overdrawn or even wrong, but they are certainly sufficiently plausible to merit serious investigation.

A decade or so ago, many political scientists joined the movement advocating metropolitan government. Their argument was that as urban areas operate as systems, social intervention requires central planning and central governing. Another wave of political scientists berated these reformers for interjecting their own values where they were inappropriate. They argued that metropolitan decentralization occurs because it is democratically chosen. It represents the way that people want to live. Who are we to tell them differently? There is certainly ample evidence to indicate that the present metropolitan settlement has very substantial support.

It has never been my view that political scientists are at their finest when they offer glosses and rationales for the *status quo,* and that is what we do when we explain political settlements by saying they are the product of people's preferences. It is when we improve on such conventional ways of explaining events that political science begins to live up to its promise.

There are a number of baseline questions which need to be asked about the American metropolitan form. Two of the most important are these: Is social-spatial segregation increasing or decreasing? Does political fragmentation affect the degree of social-spatial segregation? These questions are important because the metropolitan form provides a mechanism by which people who disagree can get away from each other, leading to both desirable and undesirable results. For example, people who care about schools often live in one suburb, and those who do not, in another. This may in fact reflect social class divisions, and we may be developing a social mechanism for creating a more rigid class structure. Without giving them different names, as do the Europeans, we create an array of schools which nearly assures differential social mobility. Furthermore, we do this in such a fashion that it is hard even to raise the issue politically because, after all, education is a local matter.

There are numerous other questions we need to be asking about the social access policies implicit in the metropolitan form. To what extent does the circulation system influence spatial specialization? Do the systems, in turn, overload because of increased spatial articulation? Is there a continual and reciprocal relation between spatial specialization and transportation overload?

Are the objects of access changing over time? Technology has made home-site choice more independent of place of work than ever before. What are the changing priorities in locational orientation? Is there greater spatial segregation of jobs of different status categories? Do people with different jobs have more or less contact than previously?

Do different areas filter down at different rates? If so, how can we explain this? Can suburban municipalities affect their economic vitality through investment policies? That is, can a proper mix of private and public investment "preserve" an area?

Do suburbs which underinvest filter down more quickly? Are filtering rates a function of location within the metropolis?

Are there differences in the political processes in varying specialized suburbs? If statements about differences in class behavior are correct, then we might expect that the differences would express themselves in political process differences among class specialized municipalities.

In intergovernmental dealings, are all types of specialized suburbs equally adept? Is there an identifiable redistributional bias to intergovernmental intervention? How valid is the thesis that state and federal governments leave the metropolitan settlement undisturbed?

What are the social and political mechanisms through which locational strategies are realized? Is location explained better by ecology or by politics? Is it a function of information and communication systems which are socially structured and coordinated? What are the symbols and cues which actors use in making choices? The daily press gives us inklings of how the system operates when values clash. One reads of a middle-class residential community harassing the owner of a psychedelic "head shop." A woman who grows corn in her front lawn is brought before the local zoning board. A suburban realtor group works out a way of classifying eligible buyers according to a variety of life style indicators, including national origin, occupation, and even grammar and swarthiness. A school teacher is fired because she criticizes American foreign policy in Viet Nam. Citizens throw black paint on the first house in a neighborhood sold to a Negro. These are certainly clear statements of a quasi-public or public definition of who is not welcome. Because the urban process does not operate simply through overt conflict, most of the urban forming actions are not newsworthy.

The core city has historically been the refuge for the oppressed, the haven for the oddball and the escapee from conformity; some would say it is the incubator of innovation. But core cities are rapidly losing their attractiveness for such persons. Core cities are instead becoming large, specialized lower class communities, if not black lower class ones. The new expanded automobile city of suburbia does not politically or socially recreate the old core city environment. While spatial specialization may seem to offer the possibility of providing a compatible community for every man, this is logically impossible, and the process of sorting out who gets the prize can get rough. The system does not guarantee that there will be a place for all, nor even a voice for all, in deciding what kinds of communities there will be from which to choose.

Structural reforms provide no easy answers for urban problems. Much that has been said above raises doubts about decentralization. There may be an implication that this book is written to advocate metropolitan government. In a way that impression is correct. But by metropolitan government we cannot simply mean the consolidation of city and suburbs. The urban form is becoming too extensive, complex, amorphous, and centerless for that. Instead it is suggested that urban politics needs to be politicized, and once the urban process becomes more political, it will probably lead to the creation of large-scale administrative units.

Nationally we are doing a great deal of hand wringing over what is to be done with urban problems. Such frustration is a symptom of not being able to formulate remedial plans based on a knowledge of how the urban system works. Political scientists need to do their part in developing this strategic knowledge. It is my personal conviction that for the United States, investigations should focus on mobility as a substitute for formal politics and the strategies and behavior of urban territorial coalitions.

Present practices place in private hands the socially important task of city building. Economic market power is translated too directly and too immediately into the priorities for urban change. The result is that we have no concept of a basic minimum or floor for urban utilities. The ghetto is the final expression of a system which can completely ignore, for some, the fact that location is an important means for achieving essential social access. As an urban phenomenon, a ghetto is the residual location which is occupied by those having the least power in the urban process. The task of social science is to understand this allocation process, so that effective strategies of social intervention can be launched.

Index